After War Times

After War Times

An African American Childhood in Reconstruction-Era Florida

T. Thomas Fortune

Edited by Daniel R. Weinfeld

With an Introduction by Dawn J. Herd-Clark
and an Afterword by Tameka Bradley Hobbs

The University of Alabama Press Tuscaloosa

The University of Alabama Press
Tuscaloosa, Alabama 354870380

Manufactured in the United States of America

Typeface: Garamond Premiere Pro
Cover photograph: Children, Jacksonville, FL, 1870s. Courtesy of the State Archives of Florida.
Cover design: Michele Myatt Quinn

∞

The paper on which this book is printed meets the minimum requirements of American National Standard for Information Sciences—Permanence of Paper for Printed Library Materials, ANSI Z39.48–1984.

Library of Congress Cataloging-in-Publication Data

Fortune, Timothy Thomas, 1856–1928.
After war times: an African American childhood in reconstruction-era Florida / T. Thomas Fortune; edited by Daniel R. Weinfeld; introduction by Dawn J. Herd-Clark; afterword by Tameka Bradley Hobbs.
pages cm
Includes bibliographical references and index.
ISBN 978-0-8173-1836-9 (cloth: alk. paper) — ISBN 978-0-8173-8767-9 (e book) 1. Fortune, Timothy Thomas, 1856-1928—Childhood and youth. 2. African Americans—Florida—Jackson County—Biography. 3. African Americans—Florida—Jackson County—Social conditions—19th century. 4. Reconstruction (U.S. history, 1865-1877)—Florida—Jackson County. 5. Jackson County (Fla.)—race relations. 6. Fortune family. I. Weinfeld, Daniel R. (Daniel Robert), 1967- editor. II. Title.
F317.J2F67 2014
305.896'073075993—dc23 2014010538

Contents

Acknowledgments

The authors wish to acknowledge the guidance and assistance of Dr. Canter Brown Jr. The idea for this edition of *After War Times* originated with Dr. Brown's observation that T. Thomas Fortune's memoir was an invaluable but neglected classic that warranted scholarly examination and deserved broader attention. Dr. Brown's participation, however, did not cease with inspiring this project. The authors assigned Dr. Brown the role of mentor and took full advantage of his generosity with his time and expertise in the history of Florida and its African American community. This book is the result of Dr. Brown's enthusiasm and kindness.

The Clime of My Birth

Oh, take me again to the clime of my birth,
The dearest, the fairest, to me on the earth,
The clime where the roses are sweetest that bloom,
And nature is bathed in the rarest perfume!

When the songs of the birds awake us at morn
With a thrill of delight and pleasure new born;
For the mocking bird there is loudest in hymn,
With notes ever changing, none fettering him.

When the hills of the North are shrouded in snow,
When the winds of Winter their fiercest do blow—
Then take me again to the clime of my birth,
Dear Florida—dearest to me on the earth.

—T. Thomas Fortune

Dreams of Life

However we will, the impressions made upon the mind between the years of childhood and manhood color all of our future thought and effort. The home where we were born, the persons whose lives touched our own, however remotely; the public square in which we played marbles or "shinny," the ponds in which we bathed in summer, the little streams in which we fished, the fields in which we set traps for birds, the dear little church, the stately court house and the sombre jail, and the village schoolhouse—the remembrance of these abides with us in the hurly-burly of after years, however far we wander from them and whatever other associations may enter into our lives and become a part hereof.

—Timothy Thomas Fortune
from *Dreams of Life: Miscellaneous Poems,* 1905

Timothy Thomas Fortune, circa 1885. Photographs and Prints Division, Schomburg Center for Research in Black Culture, New York Public Library, Astor, Lenox and Tilden Foundations.

Introduction

Dawn J. Herd-Clark

Timothy Thomas Fortune emerged in the late nineteenth century as a powerful and eloquent spokesman for African American hopes, aspirations, and perspectives. Using the Harlem-based newspaper he operated as his pulpit, the young journalist drew wide attention and rivaled the influence of legendary individuals such as Booker Taliaferro Washington and William Edward Burghardt DuBois. But while Fortune spoke out on the issues that concerned all Americans of his time, he kept a close watch on the increasingly precarious situation of African Americans. He focused particularly on the plight of blacks in his native Deep South where the advent of Jim Crow was inexorably rolling back all the gains of Reconstruction.

The oppression of blacks in the South frustrated Fortune. He rang in the twentieth century by stirring national controversy with a clarion call for what became the Great Migration. "I propose to start a crusade," he proclaimed in June 1900, "to have the negroes of the South leave that section and to come north or go elsewhere." The native southerner continued, "It is useless to remain in the South and cry Peace! Peace! when there is no peace."[1]

Fortune's disenchantment with the South intensified with the demise of Reconstruction-era promises and the onset of Jim Crow racial discrimination and associated violence, but memories of his family life and experiences as a child and young adult in Florida echoed within his heart and mind. He had moved away from the Sunshine State in the late 1870s, but the incidents and personalities of the past remained to him vivid and compelling. Fortune shared these memories at length and in detail beginning in summer

1927, with the series "After War Times" that appeared in the *Philadelphia Tribune* and the *Norfolk Journal and Guide*. In the latter publication, an additional three articles covered his experiences in Delaware and Washington, DC, after leaving Florida. Those recollections, offered in the third person and approaching creative nonfiction, form the basis for the collection that follows.

Fortune accorded major significance to his Florida childhood, presenting his youth as key to his intellectual development. The future race leader was born on October 3, 1856, in Marianna, the seat of the north Florida county of Jackson. Bordering on southeast Alabama and the southwestern tip of Georgia, Jackson County formed the western border of the state's cotton-belt region known as Middle Florida. Old South ways predominated in a locale that only recently had emerged from conditions of raw frontier to convert into a settled plantation economy. Still, by 1860, Jackson contained over 10,000 persons, a considerable number in a state with only about 140,000 inhabitants. Nearly half of the county's population consisted of enslaved men, women, and children, while free non-whites (mostly Native Americans) added up to a mere forty-three individuals. Marianna serviced a large rural area with stores, churches, schools, and other local amenities.[2]

Within the relatively isolated world of mid-nineteenth-century Jackson County, family connections shaped young T. Thomas Fortune's life. His father, Emanuel, had been born a slave in Jackson during 1832. Emanuel's father, an Irishman named Thomas Fortune, reportedly died in a pistol duel when Emanuel was an infant. "[Thomas] was a highly educated but quick-tempered man," a report described, "and not fitted to endure the hauteur of the slave master class among whom he drifted by chance." Emanuel's mother was the progeny of, as grandson Timothy described them, "a mulatto" and "a Seminole Indian." Initially owned by the Russ family, Emanuel benefitted from a degree of fluidity in the institution of slavery in Jackson County. Historian Jerrell H. Shofner detailed instances, for example, where bondsmen were tried by local courts and found innocent, one of them freed from an accusation of murder. And, although a piece of 1828 legislation prohibited slaves from leaving plantations without written permission from owners, slaveholders routinely ignored the statute as long as relative calm prevailed in the community. Reflecting this relative toleration, Emanuel learned rudimentary reading skills through interaction with his owner's son and friend, Joseph Russ. Emanuel thereafter went on to learn the trades of shoemaker and tanner, although time would illustrate his deft command of many other talents. Not surprisingly, he would be remembered by his family as "a man of extraordinary force and gifts."[3]

The Russ family may have sold Emanuel to Marianna merchant Eli P. Moore when Emanuel married Sarah Jane Mires, a slave in the Moore's village household. Born in Richmond, Virginia, in 1833, Sarah Jane lived only to the age of thirty-two. Thomas Fortune described his mother as a "small, wiry woman, of splendid figure." Her son insisted that Sarah "was, by many, considered the most beautiful woman in Jackson county, Florida" and that she possessed "a strength of character not often found in a woman slave." Fortune's biographer Cyrus Field Adams recorded that, compared with her husband, Emanuel, Sarah "was easily the stronger and more forceful." Fortune's adoration of his mother was fierce and unfailing. According to Adams, Fortune confided that his mother was "one of the most affectionate and lovable of women, and that to her precept and example he owes more than to all the other influences which have enriched his life."[4]

The Fortune family grew in the years following Timothy's birth. The young family lived in or near Eli Moore's Marianna town home, where Sarah continued to serve the master's family. Emanuel operated "a large tannery" for his owner and continued to do so through the war years. As the violent struggle churned slowly in the direction of Jackson County, the Fortunes looked inward as their fourth child, son Emanuel Fortune Jr., endured "a severe attack of pneumonia, which at one time threatened his life." The child survived but was left for the time being "completely paralyzed on the left side." Thomas and his other siblings were compelled to assume greater responsibilities as Emanuel and Sarah attended young Emanuel as "the object of special parental care and filial affection."[5]

The Fortunes could not forever ignore the national crisis that played out beginning in 1861. Thomas had attained only the age of four when Florida left the Union to join the nascent Confederate states. During the crisis of the winter of 1860–1861, Jackson County had stood divided, with many loyal Whigs opposing secession. But with the start of the war in April 1861, local whites closed ranks and supported the Confederacy enthusiastically. Dreams of a quick and painless conflict soon gave way to casualty reports, conscription enforcement, and crop tithes. The violence and death wrought its havoc elsewhere until, in September 1864, Union forces operating from Pensacola trekked across the vast swamps and pinelands that separated Jackson County from Escambia Bay. The resulting Battle of Marianna left more than 25 percent of the village's white males dead, wounded, or captured.

Thomas noted this "great calamity" as one of his first solid memories of life, acknowledging that he "remember[ed] very little about slavery." He recorded, "[D]ead bodies and shotguns and pistols were scattered far and wide, and it was some weeks before they were gathered in—the bodies to be buried and the firearms to be treasured."[6]

The battle begins Timothy Thomas Fortune's telling of his own story in "After War Times" from childhood through his early twenties. The annotations that accompany the text in this volume will provide needed context and help to guide the reader. Appreciation of Fortune's literary achievement, however, requires illuminating the context into which Fortune's contributions fit and the influences that shaped his worldview. For example, "After War Times" fills in gaps of historical and societal knowledge. Few first-hand accounts of the African American experience in Florida during the Civil War and Reconstruction eras survive, especially one from the son of a prominent African American politician. To a large extent, the same point applies to the literature of the South generally. Our understanding of the past has been slanted toward a white perspective, intentionally so in earlier generations and more by the force of intellectual inertia in modern ones.

Fortune's starting point at the Battle of Marianna offers one of the very few instances of a Civil War event occurring in Florida that was recorded by African Americans. Coincidentally, Armstrong Purdee, born a Jackson County slave the same year as Fortune, penned in 1931 an account of the battle for the Men's Club at Marianna's St. Luke's Episcopal Church. Beyond Purdee and Fortune's accounts of Marianna, there is only Susie King Taylor's *Reminiscences of My Life in Camp with the 33d United States Colored Troops, Late 1st S.C. Volunteers*. Privately published in Boston in 1902, Taylor's book remained essentially unavailable until republished in 1988. Taylor may have been the only African American woman to publish a memoir of her wartime experiences, and her account included first-hand recollections of the 33rd USCT's Florida exploits.[7]

Susie King Taylor's memoir, however, differs markedly in approach from Fortune's "After War Times." Born eight years prior to Fortune, she grew up a slave on Georgia's coast rather than in the Middle Florida cotton belt. While Fortune at least technically remained a slave until after the war's end, Taylor was ushered safely behind Union lines by an uncle and into freedom. When the Federal soldiers learned that Taylor was literate, they asked her to teach other contrabands, as escaped slaves then were called. Throughout her narrative Taylor discusses how the United States military used her as an educator, nurse, and laundress. Her work primarily focuses on the Civil War but also gives her take on Reconstruction; Fortune's centers on Reconstruction but commences before the peace and his emancipation. While both authors discuss the importance of education during Reconstruction, Taylor provides the perspective of an African American teacher while Fortune sees things with a student's eye. Working with a white family provides Taylor an opportunity to leave the South; Fortune leaves in order to seek his fate as a leader within the emerging black intelligentsia. Finally, her book concludes with a fatalistic reflection on race relations. "I sometimes ask, 'Was the war in vain?'" she queried. "Has it brought freedom, in the full sense of the word, or has it not made our condition more hopeless?" Fortune sees the problems but refuses to concede an inevitable negative result for the race while striving to project the proper paths to take.[8]

While their approaches and attitudes may differ, Taylor and Fortune are lonely voices. They are nearly drowned out by a hurricane of correspondence, government documents, newspapers, and memoirs that mostly aim to legitimize and often glorify the southern tragedy of defeat and the subsequent all-costs resistance to the postemancipation new order that threatened the racial and political antebellum status quo. As Canter Brown Jr. has pointed out, uncovering the basic facts of the black experience during Reconstruction poses an immense challenge.[9]

Surprisingly, and somewhat contrarily, Florida played an outsized role in postwar African American intellectual and political development. Florida—specifically the African American communities of Jacksonville and Tallahassee—may claim credit for a number of pioneers of black writing during the post–Civil War era who had far-reaching influence into the twentieth century. Their numbers may have been small, but their influence proved large. Several of these individuals influenced T. Thomas Fortune, who spent much of his youth shuttling between the two cities, while others were influenced or nurtured by him.

One largely forgotten African American Floridian was John Thomas Shuften. A native of Augusta, Shuften served briefly in 1865 as editor of that city's *Colored American*, noted for being the first African American newspaper in the South "after the war." Shuften advocated civil and political equality among Georgia's freedmen but found pursuing a barber's trade more lucrative and dependable. In Augusta and later in Brunswick, he remained active in Republican affairs but, by the mid-1870s, he had moved to Jacksonville. There, Shuften worked half the year for the *Florida Union*, a white-owned newspaper that favored the Republican Party, and, during the other half of the year, pursued a law degree at Howard University. Also during this time, Shuften was preparing a lengthy and thoughtful essay on Reconstruction and its failures. When published in Jacksonville in 1877, the landmark political study carried the title *A Colored Man's Exposition of the Acts and Doings of the Radical Party of the South, From 1865 to 1876, And Its Probable Overthrow By President Hayes' Southern Policy*. Just as Fortune would grow disenchanted with the Republican Party, Shuften's disgruntled prose criticized Republican politicians' interactions with freedmen, whom he believed were being manipulated.[10]

On the other hand, Shuften could moderate his views to support certain Republicans as individuals, and that route may have been the one that brought him into contact with Fortune, when the family relocated to Jacksonville in 1869. Josiah Thomas Walls, the Republican who gained Shuften's favor, was the sole African American congressman elected from Florida during the Reconstruction era. As readers of "After War Times" will discover, Fortune points out that he served as the personal secretary to the "former Union soldier, [who] was Adjutant-General of Militia and every inch a soldier, and [who] carried his sword as a soldier to buttress the dignity of his position." Walls is also noted for being the first African American to own a newspaper in Florida, Gainesville's *New Era*. If Fortune had not already become acquainted with Shuften during his own early 1870s employment at the *Florida Union*, Walls likely provided the introductions. From the two men, Fortune would have learned with little trouble just how the press offered an easily accessible tool for helping to mobilize African Americans politically. Perhaps Shuften even had a hand in encouraging Fortune to matriculate at Howard University, when he moved to Washington in 1876, the year Shuften graduated from its law school.[11]

Shuften was not the only black Floridian known to Fortune and Walls to write about Reconstruction. Walls's fellow Union army veteran John Wallace used a teaching position near Tallahassee to launch a political career that included service in the state house of representatives and state senate, where he remained until 1881. Wallace, too, endured disenchantment with politics as usual within Republican circles and opted in the mid-1880s to express his views by producing the first published history of Florida's Reconstruction experience. Titled *Carpetbag Rule in Florida: The Inside Workings of the Reconstruction of Civil Government in Florida After the Close of the Civil War*, the volume details Reconstruction politics, often at first hand.

Wallace particularly criticizes carpetbaggers for cupidity and avarice. He asserted that the Democrats—or, at least, some Democrats—were the true political friends of freedmen, and their ascension to power was a "blessing in disguise to the colored people of Florida." In an area of personal interest to Fortune, the author additionally blames the carpetbaggers for Jackson County racial turmoil and violence during 1869 through 1871. Wallace devoted an entire chapter to that violent clash, which he entitled "The Purman-Hamilton Reign of Terror in Jackson County." Its text attributed all the brutality that took place there to provocations by the Freedmen's Bureau representatives Charles M. Hamilton and William J. Purman. According to Wallace, "Every device was resorted to by these agents to embitter the colored man against the white man." Fortune's account in "After War Times" contrasts Wallace with an extremely positive view of Purman, his old acquaintance and patron, and Hamilton, both of whom were greatly esteemed by their African American constituents. These conflicting accounts provide what may be Florida's only narrative duel of any length from African American sources regarding state events and personalities of the nineteenth century.[12]

John T. Shuften, Josiah Walls, and John Wallace clearly offered excellent role models for impressionable young Timothy Thomas Fortune, but they by no means were the only ones of a political and literary bent who lived and worked in Fortune's proximity during his youth in Florida. Another was John Willis Menard, the first African American elected to the US Congress. Illinois-born Menard had worked in the Lincoln administration before heading to New Orleans as the Civil War neared its end. Menard quickly became involved in journalism and politics and capped his local career through election in 1868 to the US House of Representatives. Denied the seat by the body's Republican majority, a disappointed Menard nonetheless emerged as the first African American to address the Congress. He relocated to Jacksonville, Florida, in 1871 with an appointment to a job in the Jacksonville post office. Menard also helped to edit the city's *Florida Sun* and quickly resumed his political activities. By the late 1870s, he was a veteran of the Florida legislature and the foremost African American journalist in the state.[13]

As Fortune came to know well, Menard's perspectives were as significant as his accomplishments. In the latter category, he claimed literary stature within the African American community by writing and, in 1879, publishing a book of poetry called *Lays in Summer Lands* that received plaudits from around the nation and served as an excellent forerunner of Fortune's 1905 volume *Dreams of Life: Miscellaneous Poems.* Shortly after the publication, Menard moved to the state's largest city of Key West and, within two or three years, had taken over as editor of the *Florida News.* Back in Jacksonville by 1886, he changed the paper's name to the *Southern Leader*, a choice suggesting his personal vision for the weight of its influence. Jerrell H. Shofner, distinguished for his insightful Florida studies, analyzed the results of the journalist's efforts. Menard was, the historian insisted, "the most influential black editor speaking for and to blacks in the 1880s." He added, "His vigorous editorials were aimed at the political, economic, moral, and educational improvement of his race."[14]

Using the power of the press, Menard spoke loudly for the rights of African American Floridians, and he, too, became disgruntled with Republican officials whom he felt manipulated African American voters. Menard and Fortune—who, by the 1880s was associated with the *New York Globe*, *New York Freeman*, and *New York Age*—offered opposing views as to how African Americans could improve their circumstances in the United States. They developed in the process a sharp but friendly rivalry that found exposure around the country. Menard proved more optimistic about the race's plight than did Fortune. However, as the quality of race relations in the United States declined, Menard saw more merit in Fortune's ideas. The two men shared many elements of experience, both being fascinated, for instance, by the political arena and by newspapers. And, like Menard, Fortune's writings touched insightfully upon contemporary issues during the Reconstruction and post-Reconstruction eras including the economic, social, and political conditions of African Americans. By addressing these issues, both authors hoped to help African Americans preserve and exercise their civil and economic rights while also illustrating for whites the intellectual capabilities of African Americans. Fortune summed up his take on his friendly rival in 1889, after yellow fever in Jacksonville had closed the *Southern Leader* and compelled Menard to take his family to Washington, DC: "Mr. Menard is a gentleman of brilliant parts," Fortune recorded, "who has had many ups and downs in life but managed always to 'keep in the middle of the road.'"[15]

Menard's and Fortune's experiences also intertwined with another prominent African American Floridian, younger than either and influenced by both. James Weldon Johnson—eventually the first executive director of the National Association for the Advancement of Colored People and author of the revered song "Lift Every Voice and Sing," sometimes called the Negro National Anthem—was born in Jacksonville in 1871, not long after the Fortune family arrived in town as refugees from Jackson County political violence. Johnson avowed what both men meant to him in his now-classic *Along This Way: The Autobiography of James Weldon Johnson*, published in 1933. Of the seemingly elderly and somewhat distant Menard, Johnson observed, "I have a very clear recollection of [him], looking a good deal like the pictures of Alexandre Dumas; he was the first Negro elected to Congress, and, when I knew him, was running a weekly newspaper in Jacksonville." Meanwhile, Johnson knew Fortune as a child, and his strongest mental picture of the man came from an acquaintance during a visit to New York in 1884. "When I went to [my friends] the Jacksons, I frequently saw T. Thomas Fortune; he lived in the same house," Johnson began. "I knew him well; he was a native of Florida and before he moved to New York was a frequent visitor at our house." He continued: "My two playmates and I were sometimes in a room where he sat at a desk writing, covering sheet after sheet that he dropped on the floor, and all the while running his fingers through his long hair. He was writing his first book, *Black and White: Land, Labor, and Politics in the South*, an economic study of the race problem." Johnson concluded, "We stood in awe of him; we had no conception of how great a man he was, though not yet thirty, and of course no thought of how much greater a man he was to become."[16]

As Fortune vividly describes in "After War Times," his youth was shaped not only by the intellectual fervor of Jacksonville but also by the political tumult of Tallahassee. Tallahassee offered young Fortune the environment that he might have dreamed of finding as the era of Radical Reconstruction dawned in the Sunshine State. There he embraced the excitement of city life. Admittedly, Florida's capital remained one of the smallest cities in a state without large municipalities. Still, state government was rooted there; politics swirled in its rooms, halls, and streets; and the conflicts and personalities of the time competed for attention. Here, the practical—and sometimes dirty—work of politics played out, and, given a front-row seat, Fortune gained exposure firsthand. Perhaps no player within the black community played a more spirited role within his sight than did state senator Charles H. Pearce of Leon County. The presiding elder of the Florida Conference of the African Methodist Episcopal Church, Bishop Pearce combined the compelling force of religion with the power of the ballot box. He served at various times as a delegate in the 1868 constitutional convention, Leon County superintendent of schools, Tallahassee councilman, and Leon County tax assessor. Although Pearce's influence waxed and waned, he still was playing a role in state and church politics twenty years later.[17]

The Baptists offered leadership in Tallahassee, but the African Methodist Episcopal (AME) Church stood at the forefront of local institutions. Many of its leaders, such as William Bradwell, served as lieutenants to Bishop Pearce. Bradwell had come from Georgia, where his brother Charles emerged as a leader in the national church organization. William achieved election to the 1868 constitutional convention representing the northeast section of the state, then stepped into the Florida senate as Duval County's man on the scene. It was said of him, "The threats and abuse of his enemies tended to replenish his storehouse." Though Pearce enjoyed the support given by Bradwell and numerous others, he also faced challenges to his leadership. From such instances Fortune clearly would have divined weaknesses as well as strengths in the democratic structure then emerging. Robert Meacham, son of a Gadsden County physician and politician, ranked first in this regard. From Monticello and Jefferson County where Pearce relegated him, Meacham impacted upon the state senate and narrowly missed election to Congress. Ultimately he left the AME Church but never abandoned his leadership role until a white policeman seriously wounded him in Tampa in the 1890s.[18]

Of course, Fortune did not limit his Tallahassee exposure to politicians representing church organizations. That was not the path taken by Walls or even by Presbyterian minister Jonathan Gibbs. A good example of that sort of man was Henry S. Harmon, a Pennsylvania-born soldier who ended up in Gainesville and Alachua County. Taking public office for the first time in 1867 as a voter registrar, he followed with his election to the Florida house of representatives in 1868. Ultimately, Harmon became the first and only African American to serve as that body's speaker. Maintaining power in Republican circles into the 1880s, Harmon eventually moved to Tallahassee where he died in 1889 around the twentieth anniversary of his history-making effort to become the state's first black lawyer. This man suggested vividly to Fortune and many others the substance of his race's emerging influence in Florida and in its social and professional fabric.[19]

There were other Floridians who could be mentioned as influences on the young Fortune, but these examples from Jacksonville and Tallahassee make the point: Fortune emerged from a special Florida environment that encouraged creative expression and political reflection. This was mighty company with which to stand. Given the intellectual power that they and their associates—men such as Menard's son-in-law Thomas Van Renssalaer Gibbs and Johnson's partner in the *Jacksonville Daily American* Milton J. Christopher—brought to the table, it would have seemed natural to press the very limits of craft and mind to address the monumental problems of the time and to create beauty and perfection of expression through poetry and prose. No wonder that Fortune kept his memories of Florida so close and wanted to share them before his death.[20]

The importance of "After War Times," however, is not solely to memorialize the African American Floridians who influenced Fortune's intellectual development. Fortune's eyewitness account is a crucial document for understanding Reconstruction. Conservative whites had controlled the record of the post–Civil War era largely as a result of the absence of contrary testaments. John Wallace may have published the first history of Florida Reconstruction during the late 1880s, but white scholars have been writing Reconstruction history from within a racial tunnel since its conclusion. The first comprehensive historical inquiries on the subject set the trend that resisted breaking for at least two generations. These efforts derived from the work and mentorship of Columbia University's William Archibald Dunning. Dunning, as well as his cadre of students—including William Watson Davis, author of *The Civil War and Reconstruction in Florida* (1913)—generally wrote as if freedmen did not deserve political rights, the Ku Klux Klan was an organization that gallantly protected southern whites from freedmen, and as a class of low society carpetbaggers and scalawags simply were corrupt. Black sociologist W. E. B. DuBois attempted to challenge this train of thought in his *Black Reconstruction In America*, published in 1935. The scholar successfully placed African Americans at the center of Reconstruction, but his race and Marxist interpretation led most white historians of the southern experience to turn away from his arguments until the civil rights era of the 1950s and 1960s. DuBois's work thereafter directly or indirectly influenced many historians, especially of the younger generation, causing them to further reexamine the time period and reach markedly different opinions than had the Dunning School. Such studies on Florida included Joe M. Richardson's *The Negro in the Reconstruction of Florida, 1865–1877*, Jerrell H. Shofner's *Nor Is It Over Yet: Florida in the Era of Reconstruction, 1863–1877*, and Edward C. Williamson's *Florida Politics in the Gilded Age, 1877–1893*.[21]

But even these latter-day historians suffered from the nature of available source materials. Fortune's first-hand account of Reconstruction does make a difference by countering the prevailing views. One significant example of Fortune's contribution is his consideration of the Freedmen's Bureau. The Bureau of Refugees, Freedmen, and Abandoned Lands was created by Congress at President Abraham Lincoln's urging in March 1865, as a mechanism to address various issues throughout the South as the former Confederate states attempted to rejoin the Union. In Jackson County, Florida, the Freedmen's Bureau provided much-needed aid for local freedmen. Since Jackson barred blacks from education prior to the Civil War, the Freedmen's Bureau provided the principal means for making educational opportunities available for the area's former slaves. While Joe M. Richardson's pioneering work "The Freedmen's Bureau and Negro Education in Florida" details the efforts of the Bureau in Florida based principally on official correspondence and reports, Fortune's work provides the priceless perspective of a student in one of the state's Freedmen's schools. It affords a meaningful sense of the experience, highlighting articulately the great vigor with which freedmen pursued an education.[22]

In addition to education, freedmen pursued politics to advance their causes, especially once they attained suffrage rights. When Florida's African American male population received the franchise in 1867, the newly qualified voters, not surprisingly, began to elect African Americans to political office. As noted earlier, Canter Brown Jr.'s *Florida's Black Public Officials, 1867–1924*, utilizes a variety of primary sources to explore many of the African American elected officials in Florida, elaborates on who these politicians were, and discusses their numerous accomplishments attained despite the odds they faced. His principal autobiographical source from within the state's black community was "After War Times."

Fortune offered a unique view of what it was like to be the child of one of these African American elected officials and to have been involved as a young person with politicians and politics. Fortune's father Emanuel, the former skilled slave and AME church layman, had been appointed to the county board of voter registration, was elected one of four officials to represent Jackson County at the Florida Constitutional Convention of 1868, and subsequently served in the Florida house of representatives. In the 1870s he sat as a Duval County commissioner and city marshal, followed by a stint as a Jacksonville councilman in the late 1880s. Fortune explored from memory political topics freedmen addressed during Reconstruction, including the election of delegates to state constitutional conventions, the harassment

African American elected officials faced when they exercised their United States constitutional rights, and the involvement of African Americans in the spoils system. As a bonus for Brown, "After War Times" also elaborated on how a former slave became a page for the Florida legislature. This is the material a good historian dreams of finding.[23]

Fortune's account also impacts our understanding of the racial and political violence of the Reconstruction era. As freedmen improved their circumstances through education, hard work, and politics, violence against them and their supporters by area whites became common in parts of Florida and especially Jackson County. Daniel Weinfeld's *The Jackson County War: Reconstruction and Resistance in Post–Civil War Florida* constitutes the first book-length text to explore the topic, detailing the atrocities committed by southern Regulators against the freedmen. Fortune's "After War Times" made the difference in permitting Weinfeld to detail the tumultuous era. Among specific violent encounters addressed in "After War Times" were the otherwise hazy murder of one-time slave John Gilbert by a former Confederate soldier and the murder of freedmen at an AME Church picnic. Although congressional reports and newspaper articles furnished Weinfeld with valuable information, his principal source from within the black community was Fortune.

Violence touched the Fortune family directly. When it escalated in the Florida Panhandle in 1869 and 1870, some officials resigned or relocated elsewhere in the state. Emanuel Fortune eventually left Jackson County in May 1869 due to hostility aimed at his political activities. According to the elder Fortune, "There got to be such a state of lawlessness and outrage that I expected that my life was in danger at all times." Fortune also received information that should he remain in Jackson County, he "would be missing some day and no one would know where [he was]." Fortune heeded the threats since he had witnessed shootings and killings. When the Fortunes left the area, it was intended to be a temporary move; however, their new home in Jacksonville soon became permanent. In that more-hospitable environment, Emanuel managed to keep his life while serving honorably as a public official and engaging lucratively as a businessman. The move brought his son to the excellent Stanton Institute for schooling and to work at the *Florida Union*. A new world and destiny had opened to young Tim Fortune.[24]

Timothy Thomas Fortune's career unfolded after he left Florida and his "After War Times" narrative concludes with his departure from Howard

University. During his time at Howard, Fortune gained more newspaper experience and exposure to the world of African Americans by working for the *People's Advocate* and entering the social circle of Frederick Douglass. The combination of political exposure and newspaper experience led to his establishing the *New York Globe* in 1881, which became a leading newspaper of the time by encouraging African Americans to fight for their civil rights. The *Globe* morphed over time into the *New York Freeman* and then the *New York Age*. Through his writings Fortune remained politically active, exploring African American self-help through the formation of the National Afro-American League, educational opportunities for all Americans, the protection of African American womanhood, and efforts to end the practice of lynching.

Because of his experiences and accomplishments and because its existence is so precious relative to the paucity of similar original sources, Fortune's "After War Times" is an invaluable memoir that helps provide a more complete picture of a vitally important period in Florida, southern, and United States history. It was to be his last major achievement. Upon his death in June 1928, one respected African American newspaper spoke for countless others when it headlined, "One of the Greatest Editors of Our Race—Passes Into the Great Beyond." It added, "In the death of T. Thomas Fortune, the race loses one of its greatest men."[25]

Editor's Note

In 1899, Joel Chandler Harris, one of the nation's most popular writers, published *The Chronicles of Aunt Minervy Ann.* Harris's novel purported to depict colorful incidents in the lives of an elderly African American couple and their white employers and neighbors in a small Georgia town in the wake of the Civil War. T. Thomas Fortune, recognized as one of the preeminent African American public intellectuals and journalists, read *The Chronicles of Aunt Minervy Ann* and recoiled at its contents. Where Harris's white readers found nostalgia and sentimentality, Fortune found caricature and belittlement. Determined to correct the book's distortions, Fortune wrote to his close associate, Booker T. Washington, that "[t]he only way we can meet this sort of thing is to go into fiction and do it. . . . [M]y 'After War Times' will be an eye opener."[1]

To understand Fortune's concept for "After War Times" and his visceral reaction to Harris's novel, it is necessary to examine *The Chronicles of Aunt Minervy Ann* and that story's close, although coincidental, parallels with the Fortune family's history. Like Harris's famous Uncle Remus stories, *The Chronicles of Aunt Minery Ann* is a work of humor. In *The Chronicles of Aunt Minervy Ann*, however, Harris departs from his familiar genre of folk tales and instead aspires toward verisimilitude to describe supposedly typical experiences and daily interactions between the races after the Civil War. Harris does invoke the economic insecurity, political awakening, and terror experienced by African Americans in the South during Reconstruction, but he sentimentalizes the challenges and lampoons the threats. The ultimate effect of *The Chronicles of Aunt Minervy Ann* is to convey the longing of the author and his white audience for the restoration of a static racial hierarchy in which considerate patrician whites preside over loyal, grateful, and subservient blacks.

He wore a blue army overcoat and a stove-pipe hat.

A. B. Frost Illustration from Joel Chandler Harris, *The Chronicles of Ann Minervy Ann*. Charles Scribner & Sons, 1909.

Harris depicts his eponymous character as an outspoken, opinionated, elderly former house slave with a stubborn pride and a fierce temper. In short, she is a stereotypical "Mammy" figure—selflessly devoted to the family of her former owners whose surname she shares. Often ridiculous and a source of amusement to her employers (and Harris's readers), Aunt Minervy Ann remembers her place and role, which remain unchanged long after emancipation. Her loyalty and submission are rewarded with the esteem and affection of the white family she has served for decades.[2]

Whereas Aunt Minervy Ann represents nostalgia for an idealized antebellum racial status quo, her husband, Hamp, validates the disgust of respectable white southerners for Reconstruction and Northern interference in southern mores. Harris portrays Hamp as illiterate, suspicious, timid, and dull-witted. For Harris, Hamp represents the typical politically active African American during Reconstruction. In Harris's plot, Hamp is elected to the Georgia state legislature, where he becomes a pawn of plundering carpetbaggers and their "mulatter" allies.[3] By daring to accede to the encouragement of Northern interlopers to rise above his assigned station, Hamp provokes violent counter-action. Hamp's life is threatened, but Harris portrays the Klan as comically inept and not a serious danger to anyone. Major Purdue, Minervy Ann's gentlemanly employer—her former owner—gallantly comes to Hamp's defense, easily thwarting the Klan's buffoonish plot.

It is easy to imagine how *The Chronicles of Minervy Ann* must have incensed Fortune. Despite superficial parallels, the experiences of the real African American family portrayed in "After War Times" were quite different from those imagined by Harris for his fictional creations. In stark contrast to Harris's caricature of Hamp, Emanuel Fortune, like many other African Americans who attained elected office during the Reconstruction era, was literate and politically sophisticated. Whereas Harris portrayed all carpetbaggers as rapacious exploiters of gullible blacks, Freedmen's Bureau agents William J. Purman and Charles M. Hamilton encouraged the political awakening of their black Jackson County constituents and formed affectionate, long-lasting bonds with the Fortune family. In contrast to the half-hearted, inept schemers in Harris's depiction of the Klan, the Regulators who beset Jackson County were murderous, organized, and efficient. The coincidental detail that Hamp worked in a printing office, and in one scene conveys his expertise and fondness for the printing presses, must have particularly grated on Fortune, who spent much of his youth in newspaper offices apprenticed as a printer's devil, picking up the trades of journalism and editing that later became his profession.

By the time he finally published his rejoinder to Harris nearly thirty years after it was originally proposed, Fortune had abandoned the fictionalized version and instead composed an autobiographical account of his tumultuous youth.[4] Rather than straightforward reportage, Fortune chose to write in a literary style and adopted the third-person perspective. The narrator of

"After War Times" is an omniscient father figure, who writes about "my son Timothy." But Fortune clarifies that the narrator is not the imagined voice of his true father, Emanuel. Instead, the narrator-father is the elderly T. Thomas Fortune who looks back across six decades to remember Timothy the child as the old man's "spiritual son." Fortune clarifies that "Timothy" and the narrator "have been one from the beginning. What I say of [Timothy], therefore, I say of myself."

"After War Times" is more than a memoir of a Deep South childhood marked by politics and violence. Fortune's retort to Joel Chandler Harris sensitively depicts an African American family that emerges from slavery resilient but scarred. In an emotionally charged portrait of his adored mother, Sarah Jane, Fortune shows the tragic psychological impact of slavery on a sensitive and proud woman. Stress induced by the violence of Reconstruction takes a fatal toll. Fortune's love for Sarah Jane is a recurring theme, and he writes that upon hearing the news of her premature death, "the light appeared to go out of his young life."

In contrast, Fortune's father, Emanuel, quickly rises from slavery to communal leadership. He is a pillar of strength and paragon of intellect. Although Fortune recalls that Emanuel was "never a father but always a friend and companion," Fortune's portrayal shows otherwise: upon emancipation Emanuel seamlessly assumes the patriarchical family role long forbidden to African American men. Decisive, dignified, and aggressively protective of his wife and children, Emanuel is truly the "extraordinary man" his son describes. With justifiable pride, the younger Fortune enumerates Emanuel's equally impressive achievements as a community leader, businessman, and as a father.

The editor of the *Norfolk Journal and Guide* wrote of Fortune that "fate was kind enough to spare him to complete his biography." After Fortune finished the memoir of his youth in December 1927, his health "ebbed away" and six months later he died.[5] "After War Times" did not prove to be the "eye opener" to his generation that Fortune hoped. Relegated to two African American newspapers, this rejoinder had little chance to redress the image of Reconstruction inserted into popular imagination by *The Chronicles of Aunt Minervy Ann*, "Dunning school" scholarship, and most decisively, by D. W. Griffith's 1915 blockbuster film, *The Birth of a Nation*. The distortions disseminated by those works linger until this day. Nevertheless, renewed attention to Fortune's final masterpiece rewards the reader with the rediscovery of a lost African American memoir that offers a singular and invaluable perspective on long-misunderstood events of the American experience.

A Note about the Transcription

"After War Times" was published as a weekly serial in the *Norfolk Journal & Guide* and *Philadelphia Tribune* beginning in July 1927. The first eighteen articles appeared in each newspaper, typically in the same week. The final three articles (describing Fortune's experiences after departing from Florida) appeared only in the *Norfolk Journal & Guide.* The text is transcribed from the two newspapers and appears as it does in the originals, with only a few exceptions. In a limited number of instances, where it appeared clear to the editor that spelling mistakes had resulted purely from typographical errors by the printer, correct spellings have been substituted. Similarly, minor variations sometimes appeared between the texts of the articles as printed in the *Norfolk Journal & Guide* and the *Philadelphia Tribune.* In those instances, the editor has adopted standard usage. The numbering of the articles assigned by the newspapers is inconsistent as are the article titles and section headings. In a few places, entire phrases or sentences are found in only one of the two newspapers. All such variations between the two original printings are identified by brackets and labeled NJG or PT, as appropriate.

After War Times

After War Times

A Boy's Life in Reconstruction Days

[NJG: July 16, 1927—Part I]
[PT: July 14, 1927—Birth of the Manchild]

Marianna, Jackson county, Florida, on the Chipola river, can hardly be located on the map of the United States, it is that insignificant, and the little river flows unchartered into Appalachicola bay. There are thousands of Southern villages in the country like Marianna, and they are of the first importance, in the estimation of those born in them, ranking all other villages beyond their horizon. Marianna sits upon its own seven hills and has its own turbulent river, with associations which are green in memory after the lapse of more than a half century. To our son Timothy it will always be the most beautiful and romantic of villages, simply because he was born there, although he left it when a child never to see it again but once for a few days.

Our son Timothy was born October 3, 1856, in the morning. A tropical storm threatened to destroy the log cabin in which his mother lived, and she was removed to a safer place a few hours before he came into the world—a slave child who must follow the slave condition of his mother.[1] Her name was Sarah Jane. Her mother was named Rachel, and she was sold South by the Bush-Allens of Richmond. Her father must have been a Jew. She was very small in stature, very beautiful and very high strung. Her mother, the only African in Timothy's family, must have been a handsome woman. It takes likely people to beget likely children and Timothy was a very likely child.[2]

In the year Timothy was born the Nation was in great confusion and uproar about human slavery. The conflicting forces were fronting each other in a death struggle, with John Brown stirring up the fighting spirit and Chief Justice Roger B. Taney, in the Dred Scott Opinion of the Supreme Court, shocking the moral sense of the Nation.[3] The civil war was only four years away. The elemental storm upon the birth of Timothy seems to have harmonized in some sort with the storm of human passion aroused over the slavery controversy. It may also have been premonitory of the stormy life Timothy was to live and in which he was to play a childish part, often weird in its lights and shadows. The childhood of the man is reflected always in the manhood of the child. The birth and childhood of Frederick Douglass, like those of Abraham Lincoln, were enveloped in mystery and tragedy, and these were strongly reflected in their temperaments and work as among the greatest and most useful men the Nation has produced.[4]

Timothy was my spiritual son. He and I have been one from the beginning. What I say of him, therefore, I say of myself. Emanuel, who begat us was never a father but always a friend and companion. He was an extraordinary man and played a very conspicuous part in the Reconstruction politics of Florida. He served as a member of the Constitutional Convention and the first four sessions of the legislature authorized by that convention.[5] He was born of an Indian mother and an Irish father. His mother was, so tradition has it, the wife of Osceola, who was stolen from Micanopy and taken to West Florida, by Thomas Fortune, an Irish adventurer, who thus caused the long and bloody Seminole war, which was brought to a close by General Andrew Jackson who conquered Osceola, near Marianna.[6] Osceola lost his life while seeking to recover his wife, who had been stolen and kidnapped.[7] She had three children, two daughters and a son, for Fortune. After his mysterious death she was taken to wife by John Pope, who was also of mixed Seminole blood. He was one of the best and cleanest men I ever knew. His wife, Docia, gave him three sons and a daughter, but they resembled in nothing the two daughters and son she gave Thomas Fortune. He raised them all with such care as he could under the circumstances, and they all loved and reverenced him.[8]

Two of John Pope's sons, Madison and Hammond, ran away and joined the Union army and fought for the freedom of their race all through the civil war. Madison settled in Boston after the war and came back to visit the old folks and childhood scenes once. He remained but a short time and then went back to Boston and we never heard from him again. Hammond faded from the family picture after he joined the army.

The family picture I have drawn is a familiar one among the millions

Osceola—Seminole leader. Artist: George Catlin, 1838. Prints and Photographs Division, Library of Congress, LC DIG-pga-00467.

produced out of the loose morality of the system of slavery. In my family there was the African, the Indian and the Jewish women and the Irish and half-breed Indian man, with the Jewish grandfather guilty of selling his daughter by the black woman into slavery in the same villages where he was a judge. I know, and so does Timothy, that when these race crosses meet in the flesh and fight for control of the one body common to them, he has to be a superman indeed, who spiritually conquers and is able to assert his mastery of "the house not made with hands, eternal in the heavens."[9]

The people responsible for the cross of the black, white and red races in this country are in very interesting and questionable business when they draw the race and color line on the sisters and brothers whom their fathers and grandfathers mulattoized. If they hope to do so and get away with it they ignore the spiritual responsibility they voluntarily assumed when they accepted Abraham for Father and the Bible for spiritual law.

The manchild, Timothy, came to life in a fierce storm of rain, thunder and lightning, and when the Nation was agitated in every state to the fighting point on the question of slavery and the aggressions of the Slave Power on the privileges and immunities, the reserved rights, of the Free States. It was not a small thing I have found, to have been born in such a confusion of the elements and of human passions, and we shall get something of a bird's eye view of the development of the Afro-American of today out of slavery and Reconstruction days and horrors, as we go along with Timothy from 1865 to 1874, when his years as a manchild came to an end in the Magic City of Washington, and his life as a human began.

[NJG: July 23, 1927—Part II]
[PT: July 21, 1927—Part Two]

Slap in the Face and Flight

I don't know just how old Timothy was when his mother was sold to Ely P. Moore, a merchant of Marianna. Moore and his wife were a very kindly disposed couple and treated Sarah Jane and her children with unusual consideration; so also did their three daughters and son.[10] The children were playmates and there was little in their treatment to show that they and Timothy and his two sisters were other than members of the Moore family. But the mother knew. The fact that she was a slave rankled in her young bosom and soured her amiable disposition, insofar that she appeared always to be discontented and restless, with seldom a smile or a laugh to indicate that life for her was other than a curse and burden. She was old enough to know and to feel, while her children were too young to realize the awful condition into which they had been born.

Timothy remembers very little about slavery. His first awakening was early in the civil war, when Confederate soldiers from all parts of Florida west of the Chattahoochie river gathered in and marched out of Marianna, many of them never to return. It appeared to the youngster that they made a brave and handsome showing, but there was no happiness shown by any of them. They realized that they were engaged in a very serious business.[11] Soon after these soldiers passed on to face death in a hopeless cause Timothy picked up a big bunch of Confederate paper money. He did not know

Florida family in front of their log cabin, 1870s. Courtesy of the State Archives of Florida.

the value of it but he knew that it had value, and he promptly turned it over to his mother, who turned it over to Mr. Moore. Timothy possessed a very large bump of honesty and it grew larger with his years. Some are born honest and can't help it while others are born dishonest and can't help it, and the honest are often victimized and undone by the dishonest.

And, then a great calamity came upon Marianna and the old and youthful white ones who were not eligible to go to the front. They were the home guard. When it was rumored that a detachment of Union soldiers was marching on the village the home guard got together and determined to repel the invaders. The battle was short, sharp and decisive. The home guard was routed. [NJG: "A great"] many of them were killed, and all the countrysides were in mourning. Dead bodies and shotguns and pistols were scattered far and wide, and it was some weeks before they were [NJG: "gathered in—the bodies to be"] buried and the firearms to be treasured.[12]

I don't know unto this day what the provocation was, but one afternoon, a few weeks after the Yankees passed through, Mr. Moore called Timothy into the Big House and was giving him a good thrashing, the first he had ever given him, when his mother came on the scene, long hair flying and eyes flashing, with a big dishrag in her right hand. Without hesitation she began to belabor Mr. Moore in the face with the dishrag, giving him a rasping tongue-lashing the while for daring to strike her child! When Moore turned on her she grabbed Timothy and made her way out. She dropped the boy at the backstairs, where he continued to pierce the air with his wailings. But she did not stop. Realizing that she had done the unpardonable thing, she kept going and was soon outside the big yard and making for the hills beyond, where she was soon lost to sight. She just seemed to Timothy to fade away. Forgetting the whipping he had received he began all over to cry aloud and louder at the flight and disappearance of his mother. She went to her husband's mother's home, [NJG: "on the outskirts of the village,"] and Mr. Moore made no effort whatever to recover her.

She remained in hiding about three weeks, when it was announced that the war was at an end and that all slaves were free.[13] Uncle Tom and his good wife, the other help, filled in her place both as to service and caring for Timothy and his sisters. Uncle Tom was a real character. He weighed about 350 pounds and he was as jolly and good natured as the day is long. Everybody loved Uncle Tom.

As soon as freedom was declared Timothy's mother returned, packed her belongings and moved into a home of her own, provided by her husband, on land belonging to Joseph W. Russ, who sustained relations of close interest and sympathy with Timothy's father which I was never able to understand.[14] It proved mighty helpful in the trying times ahead. The high spirited mother freed herself before Lincoln's Proclamation reached Marianna, and she refused to remain a day in the owner's house when she was free to order her own life. She knew what the horrors of slavery were and she rejoiced, as 4,500,000 of her race did, when the word reached her that she was free.

Timothy was too young when freedom came to look into the past or future very far, but events moved rapidly in those days. He was soon to wake up and take notice of the great changes which freedom wrought, automatically in the village and its people.

The community was still under the spell of the close of the war and the freedom of the slaves. I remember, when announcement of the suicide of former Governor John Milton, one of the most respected of the white citizens and planters, was made. He was not strong enough, at his age, to face

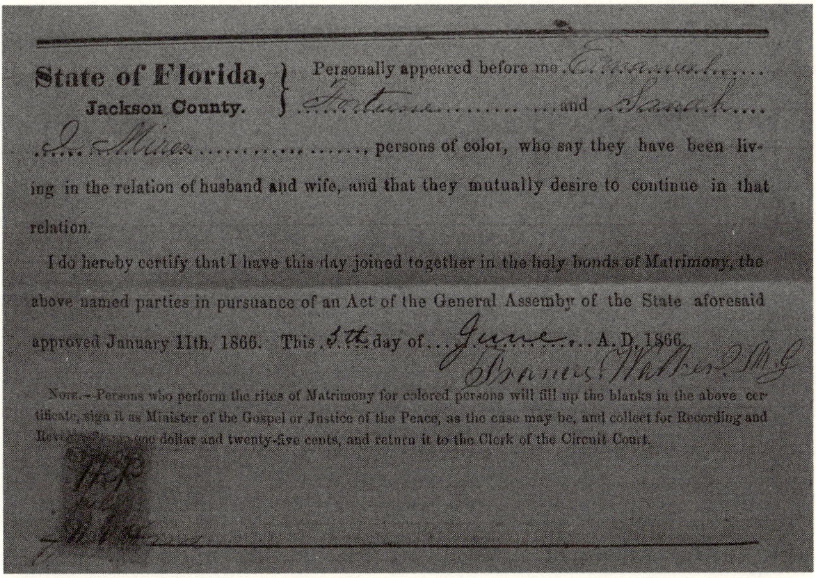

State of Florida, } Personally appeared before me Emanuel
Jackson County. } Fortune and Sarah
J. Mires, persons of color, who say they have been living in the relation of husband and wife, and that they mutually desire to continue in that relation.

I do hereby certify that I have this day joined together in the holy bonds of Matrimony, the above named parties in pursuance of an Act of the General Assemby of the State aforesaid approved January 11th, 1866. This 5th day of June A. D. 1866.

Francis Walker M.G.

Note.—Persons who perform the rites of Matrimony for colored persons will fill up the blanks in the above certificate, sign it as Minister of the Gospel or Justice of the Peace, as the case may be, and collect for Recording and Rev[illegible] one dollar and twenty-five cents, and return it to the Clerk of the Circuit Court.

Marriage Certificate of Sarah Jane Mires and Emanuel Fortune, Jackson County Courthouse, Marianna, FL.

the failure of the Confederate Cause and his own personal loss in slaves and other property. So, through all life runs the same double purpose; what brings joy and gain to some brings sorrow and loss to others.[15]

—"After War Times," continues next week with the First Reconstruction Murder.

[NJG: July 30, 1927—A Boy's Life in Reconstruction Days—Part 3]
[PT: July 28, 1927]

First Reconstruction Murder

The entire county of Jackson was upset by the close of the war and the emancipation of the slaves. Nobody had his bearings. The freed people were looking the present in the face, with new and untried responsibilities thrust upon, with no previous preparation to meet them; with no homes and no names except such as they inherited from their owners, which they very generally adopted. They were in such a frame of mind as not to know whether to rejoice and be glad because they were free at last or to be sorrowful and cast down at their new condition of freedom, responsibility, and homelessness. They were just like so many children thrown upon their own resources. Nothing could be more pathetic. It would take them sometime to realize what had befallen them.[16]

The Negro population of Jackson county was not very large.[17] The plantations were large but not numerous, and a community of interest subsisted between them which was intimate, as far as owners and slaves were concerned, the owners marrying among themselves and the slaves doing the same after the rules governing their sexual alliances. These intermarriages, had resulted in most of the whites being related to each other, with the same thing happening to the slave people; the latter having, withal, a large cross of the original Indian and Spanish in the African ground work of them. They were a very intelligent and self-reliant lot. Very few of them had been sold out of the county and few new ones had been brought into it. At the close of the civil war, therefore, nearly all of the whites were related by marriage and all of the freed people were related in the same way by the loose slave relations they had contracted. When the Freedmen's Bureau of the Federal Government was established among them shortly after the close of the war, the slave marriages were legalized by the Federal officer commanding the district. Most of the freed people took immediate advantage of the opportunity to legalize their unions. We have yet in our family the Bible furnished by the Bureau in which the marriages and births were properly entered by the Federal officer.[18]

If the close of the war and the coming of freedom had demoralized the freed people and made them anxious and uncertain of the present and the future, it had demoralized the whites far more. The Lost Cause was dear to them, and their slave and other property was affected disastrously by the defeat of the Confederate armies.[19] The richest of them found themselves reduced to poverty, with their slave property confiscated and their landed property depreciated beyond calculation by the loss of their slave labor. No wonder that most of them were made sour and vindictive by their great losses and the changed relations of master and slave.

But none of these things affected Timothy in the least. He was conscious that a radical change had taken place in his life but he was too young and inexperienced to analyze the change or to allow himself to be worried.

And then, as if a thunder bolt had descended out of a clear sky, the Marianna people were thrown into a very high state of excitement. Something had happened which had never happened in Jackson county, a thing no one dreamed possible, so even and smooth had the relations of the people theretofore been. A former Confederate soldier, a stranger in the county, had shot to death young John Gilbert, a popular Negro, on the common highway. Gilbert had a load of wood, drawn by a stout team, coming to town, when he was confronted by Sergeant Barnes, who commanded him to turn out of the road. This he did, as far as possible but it did not satisfy the sergeant who, cursing like a trooper, drew a service revolver, and shot the young man to death in cold blood.[20]

The news of the tragedy swept through the county like a prairie fire. Negro men and women from every direction swarmed into the village, fighting mad and determined to be avenged. The village and nearby swamps and forest were thoroughly searched for the bloody miscreant, all of the afternoon and the night, but he eluded capture. It was good for him that he did, as the Negroes were outraged and thoroughly aroused and would have torn him from limb to limb if they captured him. It proved a great pity that they failed, as this one man eventually organized the worst elements of the young whites of the county and in the course of time brought about a horrible reign of terror. His organization became a part of the Ku Klux Klan organization in West Florida, and if he had been caught and slain when the Negroes were determined to avenge his murder of young Gilbert, it is possible no such organization would ever have gained a foothold in Jackson county. One bad man can easily corrupt a whole community; so also one good man can often convert a wicked community from the errors of their ways. The bad man often has the courage of his convictions while the good man seldom has the courage of his and is often dragged into the wrongdoing and destroyed by his cowardice.[21]

The murder of young John Gilbert and the fierce uprising of the Negro people in their wrath made a wonderful impression on the budding mind of Timothy.

"After War Times" continues next week with the "Soldier School Masters."

Part 4
The Soldier School Masters
[NJG: August 6, 1927]
[PT: August 11, 1927]

The people of Jackson county reacted but slowly to the new conditions, and they are to be pitied rather than blamed that the Negroes had more trouble in getting their bearings than the white people. They had been expecting freedom for a long time, and praying for it as they expected, but when it came to them of a sudden they were so surprised and stunned that they did not know what to do with it. The changed attitude of the white people towards them, the hostility which was everywhere evident, gave them a great deal of concern. The readjustment of their labor relations was a problem with which they were in no wise prepared to cope, and yet it was the one which forced itself upon them most persistently.

They were in the midst of their troubles when a detachment of Union soldiers was quartered among them. This was a very great event. It angered and embittered the whites, and made them feel all the more keenly the stubborn fact that they were a conquered people. Their attitude towards the soldiers in blue was pronouncedly antagonistic. They would have no fellowship whatever with the officers or the soldiers. Colonel Charles M. Hamilton and Major William J. Purman had charge of the detachment. They were very superior men and played a conspicuous and honorable part in the Reconstruction politics of Florida. They made friends with the Negro people of course, and the few white loyalists, but to all intents and purposes, socially, they were proscribed and ostracized, and remained so to the end. It was that way with the Union soldiers and the whites in every community where the former were assigned to duty. They represented the Union government in preserving law and order, and in the proper adjustment of the labor relations of the former master and slaves, and they had charge of the important work of the Freedman's Bureau. They furnished Bibles to all the Negro people who wished to have them, and they remarried all the Negro men and women who had contracted slave unions and desired to have these legalized. Few, indeed, failed to avail themselves of the chance to do this.[22]

Another important event was the opening of the Freedman's school in the Negro church. Sergeant Smith and Private Davenport were detailed to the work of teaching the little black and colored children their first lessons in the rudiments of an education.[23] Strange to say, a large number of young Negro women also attended the school. The teachers were splendid men and the children simply idolized them. Indeed, to the Negro people the Union soldiers and their splendid officers, appeared to have been sent directly from heaven to help them in their troubles. Perhaps it was so. The school was crowded with anxious and eager pupils from the beginning, and the teachers had very smooth sailing, as all of their pupils were nervously anxious to master Webster's blue back speller. There are many living to-day

William James Purman (1840–1928). Brady-Handy Collection, Prints and Photographs Division, Library of Congress, LC-DIG-CWPBH-03733.

who remember the little blue back speller from which they got their first start in mastering an education in small or great measure.[24]

My son Timothy was as eager and apt a pupil as any of the others. He soon got the book learning fever, as many others did, and he seemed to absorb naturally the rudiments of learning. He soon became a favorite of the teachers as well as of his school mates. He had the winning way about him, and he had a knack of leading the others in school work and the childish pastimes of those days, in which marbles played a leading part. And he could "shoot" marbles some more. He was also a good fisherman and huntsman, and flying the kite and building traps for birds appeared to come natural to him.

The soldiers had dress parade twice a day, morning and evening, and all the urchins of the village were on hand to watch it. They thought it was the grandest thing ever, and it was as far as they were concerned. They were transported by the drum beating and bugle blowing. Such music they never dreamed of. And what heroes were the drummer boy and the bugler to them. The drummer boy was a son of the Sergeant Smith who had charge of the Freedman's school. He and Timothy became fast friends, but he was a favorite of all the pupils of the school.

There were no public school systems in the South before the Reconstruction governments made them possible. The whites had an academy in most of the counties, to which those who could afford the luxury sent their children.[25] The vast number of poor white people, who owned no slaves and who lived a hand-to-mouth existence, grew up in ignorance. These poor whites, who had nothing to lose and nothing to gain by the outcome of the civil war, made up the larger part of the Confederate armies. They venerated the white aristocratic class, and class it was, and hated the slaves, although there was a great deal more social intercourse between the two races than is generally known or believed. The slaves were in a position to render these poor whites, especially the poor women, many services, and during the war period, when the men were away fighting to perpetuate slavery, their wives and daughters were often supplied with food without which they would have gone hungry or starved. It was this way in Marianna, and remained so some years after the close of the civil war, as many of the husbands and sons of the poor women fell in battle and were never more heard of.

The bugle call of the soldiers for afternoon drill and parade was heard for miles around and was the first and sweetest music Timothy and the other freed people had ever heard. Have they heard any sweeter since? I doubt it.

Next week, "Cotton Picking and Tragedy."

[NJG: August 13, 1927—A Boy's Life In Reconstruction Days—Part 5]
[PT: August 18, 1927—"Cotton Picking and Tragedy"]

The drummer boy, Johnny Smith, was a sturdy little fellow. He had much experience far beyond his few years. Indeed, what he had gone thru as a drummer boy gave him experience that easily made him wise and hard as a man. He was an inveterate tobacco chewer, consuming great quantities of the "army plug," a very black tobacco saturated with molasses. Some readers of this article may remember it. Johnny soon taught Timothy the use of it, and for many years after he was a confirmed addict. It is a very difficult habit to get rid of, like most other hurtful habits so easily acquired.

It is worth while to make a note of the fact that most men were tobacco chewers and most women were snuff users in the days of slavery and long after. Many were inveterate pipe smokers, and they smoked "plug," the raw product, and often very rank. The syrup soaked "plug" the Union soldiers introduced became very popular in the South, but its popularity has long passed, and finer tobaccos, scientifically treated, have taken its place. Tobacco chewing is a very nasty habit, which few people now indulge in. Timothy's use of tobacco was hurtful to him and I am sure he would have been much the gainer if the Union drummer boy had never taught him to use it. I endeavored to dissuade Timothy from the use of it, but without success. Youth must be served. What appears good to the grownups the youngsters will hanker after. If denied it in public they will "sneak" it in private. If the grown-ups don't want the youngsters to contract bad habits they must not set them the example.

Johnny Smith undertook to tattoo the Union flag on Timothy's arm, but the process was too painful and Timothy rebelled. He was prone to rebel against anything that did not dovetail with his feelings and desires. One day Johnny gave Timothy a lot of the big brass caps used in the old army guns, and Timothy was feverishly anxious to hear them explode. Just how to make them do so puzzled him for a time. Then he hit upon the idea of placing a cap on the head of an ax, the blade of which was stuck in the earth, and striking the cap with a hammer. The experiment was a great success. The explosion was very loud and brought his mother into the yard from which the sound proceeded on the jump. Timothy was prone on the ground, writhing in pain and screaming at the top of his voice. A piece of the brass cap had struck his right knee and penetrated the flesh a full half inch. It was very painful and it was all they could do to get the piece of brass out of the wound and to prevent the development of blood poison. His mother grabbed the brass caps and made away with them. It was some days before Timothy could be up and about some other mischief.

The Negro church of Marianna had no regular pastor, but a "supply" was furnished in Rev. John Pope, Timothy's adopted step-grandfather and a Sunday school had been organized. Timothy being among the brightest of the bunch was made superintendent but he did not know and did not remain on the job long enough to find out what it was all about. With the assistance of the grownups, they and the children having entered whole-heartedly into the Sunday school work, a picnic had been mapped out for the end of the week. It was the first picnic the Negro children had ever had planned for them and great was their enthusiasm about it. But Timothy's cousin

Florida laborers in the fields picking cotton, 1890s. Courtesy of the State Archives of Florida.

Benjamin had asked him if he wanted to go up Campbellton way to pick cotton for the week, and he had been carried away with the prospect of the outing. Late Sunday afternoon they had set out for the cotton fields, Timothy regretting to have to miss the picnic, so that they could begin work early Monday morning.

Cotton picking was great fun for the youngsters and profitable for the grown-ups. Fifty cents a hundred pounds was paid, with some pecks of cornmeal and a few pounds of fat pork allowed for ration. Timothy had his ration and he was one of the best cotton pickers in the group. One must have long fingers, with handy use of them, with an active, supple body, to be an expert cotton picker. Timothy had all of these and he made almost as much money for the week as the grown-ups. All were highly elated over the outing and the money made and returned to Marianna Saturday night on very best terms with themselves and the rest of mankind.

But, horror of horrors! What awful news awaited their homecoming! The picnic had been a remarkable success in numbers and enthusiasm. All were gathered at the picnic grounds and enjoying to the full their first experience of the kind, when a party of white hoodlums, hidden in the surrounding forest, opened a deadly fire with shotguns on the women and children and the very few men in the gathering. It was ghastly business, one of the most fiendish outrages of Reconstruction days. The ground was littered with dead and maimed children and grown-ups. Sergeant Barnes and his band were credited with the unheard of barbarity but responsibility for the crime was never fixed. None of the assassins had been seen and there was no county government as yet to undertake to investigate and fix the responsibility.[26]

In this as in many other instances, Timothy appeared to bear a charmed life. His acceptance of the invitation to spend the week up country picking cotton rather than wait and attend the picnic, saved his life, possibly, as a youngster about his own age was shot to death at the very spot which Timothy always selected to occupy when fishing in that section of the country.[27]

Can you imagine a party of grown-up white persons deliberately shooting into a crowd of Sunday school teachers and children?

[NJG: August 20, 1927—A Boy's Life In Reconstruction Days—Part 6 War among School Children] *[PT: August 25, 1927—"Cotton Picking and Tragedy"]*

The population of Marianna resided mostly to the eastward, of the village and there was no segregation of the races. People lived where they could secure what they desired. All of the houses were of pine lumber [PT: "construction, a"] few on the outskirts being constructed of logs, and generally known as "log-cabins." Most of the houses were built on the one-story plan. Additions to the house were made as they were needed by family increase or otherwise. A few of the houses occupied by the merchants and professional whites, who were restricted in number, were imposing edifices, with spacious front yards, in which all sorts of beautiful flowers were cultivated, and large back yards called gardens, in which all the vegetables required by the owners, were raised in abundance. It is quite wonderful how much vegetables can be grown on a small plot of land. And it is remarkable what a leading part vegetables can play in supplying the table and cutting down the cost of living.

Fresh meat was a luxury, seldom indulged in except on Sunday, and then it usually consisted of fresh fish caught by some member of the family on Saturday, or fowls of some sort, a great variety of which were raised. Most of the village people owned a cow or two and had all the milk and butter needed and at first hand. Corn meal pone, cooked in many ways, all of them good, salt pork and cabbage, or turnip tops, and sweet potatoes, "yams" that make the mouth to water by thinking of them, so sugary sweet were they, made up the ration of the average family. There was also plenty of molasses and raw sugar, grown by the farmers and sold for a song to the village people. And there was plenty of fruit,—apples, peaches, plums and grapes,—and everybody had a grape arbor. Everybody had plenty to eat and it did not cost much. Those who had plenty were always ready and willing to divide with those so unfortunate as to have but little. All this was after war times and during several years following.

Country people are more neighborly and helpful to each other than city people. They are all friends or relatives and borrow from one another without ever expecting any pay back except in kind. A child would often trudge five miles to Timothy's home, on arriving saying:

"My mah say will you please loan 'er a peck o' meal and a bit o' salt 'twill daddy cum home."

Daddy would be away in some other part of the county working on a job and might be gone a week or many weeks. But the "paying back" was always considered a form of words and meant nothing.

The white academy had been closed during the civil war, and the white children did not have any school to go to. The academy opened about the same time the church opened for school for the Negro children under the soldier school masters. Bad feeling was shown at once by the white children. As the colored children had to pass the academy to reach the church, it was easy for the white children to annoy them with taunts and jeers and with commands that they go round another way to reach their school. Bitter words become common with both colors, and it was easily to be seen that a bad situation was being developed.

The colored children were not disposed to accept without resenting it the attitude of the white children towards them and in a war of words they were so much at home as the white children. The war passed from words to pebbles and stones, which the white children began to hurl at the colored children. Several of the latter had been struck and badly hurt by the flying stones, and as they had not resented the rock and stone throwing in kind, because they were timid about going that far, the white children became more aggressive and abusive, taking it for granted that the colored children were too cowardly to fight. In this they were mistaken.[28]

One morning soon after the rock throwing had been started by the white children, the colored children gathered on the outskirts of the village, some distance from the academy, with their school on the other side, and showed

Florida schoolchildren, 1870s. Courtesy of the State Archives of Florida.

a disposition to be afraid to pass the academy. Timothy came along about this time and took the lead in urging his school fellows to go on to their school, and to fight hard if necessary. All the pupils, at Timothy's suggestion, armed themselves with stones of all sizes, and determined to fight their way past the academy to their school.

The colored children approached the academy in mass formation whereas in the past they had been going by it in pairs or small groups. Timothy was in the front of his group, when they reached hailing distance of the academy half dozen white boys rushed out and hurled their missiles, acting as if they expected to stampede their opponents. Instead of scampering away, however, the colored children not only stood their ground and hurled their missiles, but maintained a solemn silence. The white children then, seeing there was no backing down and scampering, as they expected, came rushing out of the four sides of the academy, and charged the colored children, who stood their ground stubbornly. During some fifteen minutes it was a real tug of war between them, with little ground given by either side. In the close fighting the colored children got the advantage, gradually, and began to shove the white children back, and as they pressed the advantage, the white children broke away and ran for the academy. The colored fighters did not follow them but made it hot for the laggards until they also took to their heels.

When the scrap was about ended a white boy named Gotier, emerging from behind one of the big oaks on the academy grounds, hurled a small cobble stone, which struck Timothy on the lower part of the spine and threw him down flat.[29] It was many years after, before Timothy ceased to feel and suffer from the chance shot of the enemy. There were many bruised on both sides, but none seriously, but it taught the white youngsters to leave the colored ones alone thereafter. They had enough fighting and never interfered again with the free going and coming of the colored school children. The scrap was regarded as a children's affair by the grown-ups, and ended at that. But I have a mind that the white grown-ups with the uprising occasioned by the murder of young Gilbert still in their minds, were uncertain about the free Negro and advised their children to leave the colored children alone.

Next week "The Gravey and Possum."

[NJG: August 27, 1927—A Boy's Life In Reconstruction Days—Part 7]
[PT: September 1, 1927]

The Graveyard 'Possum

The Christmas holidays had always been among the most gala for the young and old folks of the country districts of the county, as it was the time of year when the sugarcane was ground and the animals were slaughtered for the year. "Cane grinding time" appealed to the youngsters as a holiday full of sweets, and the older ones also took part and rejoiced in the hunting of the opossum and other wild game, mostly at night, and fishing. Many of the youngsters of the village had been allowed to go up-country and spend the Christmas holidays with relatives on the plantations but Timothy had never been allowed to do so, as he was too young. The second Christmas week after freedom he was allowed to do so. He had grown to be a very wide-a-wake youngster, very much alive to country life and its many pastimes, which he had watched with his developing years and yearned to share to the full.

"Christmas-time Opossum Hunt." *Harper's Magazine*, January 1881.

He went to the Russ plantation, where he had a lot of kinfolks and where he was very much at home.[30] He stopped with Uncle John and there were plenty of children with whom he could make merry. The country eating was the best possible, with plenty of fish and wild game, and he never got his full of chewing cane and drinking hot syrup,—raw brown sugar, the only sort in common use in those days,—and what youngster did get his fill of such! Fishing in the many ponds and small streams was great sport, but the thing Timothy yearned most for was to go 'possum hunting. He had always heard that that was the greatest of things that go along with Christmas holidays.

[NJG: 'Possum Hunts Got Underway at Night]

'Possum hunts usually got underway about the midnight hour. Uncle John made up his party of six, including Timothy, the night after Timothy reached the plantation, and Timothy's first experience in hunting 'possum was begun. He was all excitement and enthusiasm and felt as frolicsome as the dogs, who do know what the sport is and take a human interest in it. Dogs have lots of sense, with no instinct about it, just as some folks have, and I have often thought that dogs may be folks but can't tell us they are, except by their actions, which are often very human.

We had not gone far from the plantation before the dogs gave the signal that they had struck a trail. It led straight to the plantation graveyard. The 'possum took to a small oak. When routed from this he took to a larger one, and then routed, he made for the largest tree in the graveyard. Uncle John decided to cut the tree down. Meanwhile the men and the dogs showed that they felt funny about the whole business from the beginning, a graveyard 'possum being regarded as a spirit and hard to capture. The dogs stood off in the direction the tree should fall, and when it fell they rushed for the prey, howling and whining in a most piteous way, but the 'possum eluded them for the third time, and Uncle John decided that was enough. His superstition took charge of him, and he was for giving up the hunt but was overruled by the others.

"Yoo cain't have no luck when you start off wid a graveyard 'possum foolin' yoo," he said, with a shake of the head.

We got up into the persimmon district of the plantation where there were plenty of opossum. The dogs jumped one of the finest which made for a clump of trees and rock, and was grabbed just as he was going into his hole. Then we had no luck for a long time, when we reached the extreme limits of the farm, and were thinking of giving up the hunt. A big one was captured at this point, and, with his tail in a split white oak limb, he was turned over to Timothy to lug. We had to cross a small stream on logs, at this point. Timothy followed the others and the dogs followed him, and kept up a constant snapping at the 'possum. Timothy struck at the dogs behind him to make them desist and the 'possum drove his teeth through the third finger and second joint of the right hand, making him turn loose the limb and 'possum. They all fell into the creek, some on one side and some on the other of the log fence. All were thoroughly drenched, and it had turned freezing cold.

We got on the other side the creek and cut a big dead pine log resin fat into sections and built a rousing fire and after awhile were dried and thawed out. Timothy's finger was very painful, and he has yet a deformity of that finger because of the bite of the opossum.

"We ain't goin' to hunt no more tonight," said Uncle John. "That graveyard 'possum done hoodoo the whole business."

He had. Although Uncle John and the others were born and reared in that part of the county, they lost their way and did not reach their plantation until broad daylight.

[NJG: September 3, 1927—A Boy's Life in Reconstruction Days—Part 8]
[PT: September 8, 1927]

The Political Agony

The free Negroes had trouble of their own, but they got a world of satisfaction out of their new relations to themselves and their white neighbors, although the latter were for the most part very reserved and cautious, as if feeling their way to a proper attitude in the new order. They could not shake off the downcast feeling which their reverses in the Lost Cause and their personal affairs cast over them. They could not realize at once that they had lost everything and faced the future empty handed, land poor in most cases with the new Negro to deal with and to keep in his place, such a place as they should decide was his, whatever he might think about it. This disposition was shown on the part of the whites in the very beginning of the Reconstruction days.

[NJG: "New Order of Government Inaugurated"]

The Constitutional Convention had been held and the new order of government inaugurated. Emanuel Fortune took a prominent part in selecting the delegates, as it was natural for him to take the leadership in any independent movement of Negroes. During and before the Civil War he had commanded his time as a tanner and expert shoe and bootmaker.[31] In such social life as the slaves were allowed and in church work he took the leader's part, and was expected to do it. When the matter of the Constitutional Convention was decided upon his people in Jackson county naturally looked to him to shape up matters for them. He visited the leading white people and invited them to join in selecting a proper delegation, but they took the position

Emanuel Fortune Sr. Courtesy of the State Archives of Florida.

that it was the business of the Negro and the carpet baggers, "the Yankee strangers," as they styled them, and they would have nothing to do with it. Mr. Fortune strove to prove to them that it was their business and to their best interest to help in making a new constitution and government on the Reconstruction plan made and provided by Congress, but they would not be convinced. The Southern whites very generally took this foolish position and made it one of the excuses for ku klux klan outrages the fact that they had no hand in creating the new order.[32]

Outrages on Negroes grew more frequent during the selection of delegates to the convention and the ensuing selection of members of the legislature. By the time the latter were voted for, and the Republicans did most of the voting, the outrages took on the nature of a terror. Mr. Fortune appealed to the responsible whites to put a stop to the outrages, but they claimed they knew nothing about them and had no knowledge or connection with those guilty of perpetrating them. Mr. Fortune, who was a dead shot and game to caution, kept to his house after dark, deeming it wise not to expose himself needlessly. And too, he had good white friends who advised him to pursue this course.[33]

[NJG: "Fortune Builds a Trap-Door Under Bed"]

Mr. Fortune built a trap door under his bed on the first floor of his house, commanding the whole front approach, and had a small arsenal in reach. The children slept in the "loft." The understanding was that, if a knock on the door came, his wife was to open the door and follow it behind as it swung, while he would drop into the trap door and, if there were persons outside, open fire on them and those of them who should rush for the house. Fortunately, for all concerned, no raid was made on him in his home, but sharp shooters sneaked about, a hundred yards away, every night.[34]

[NJG: "The Unexpected Happenings"]

And then the unexpected happened. After the whites had committed a crime against a Negro or white sympathizers in one part of the county, some prominent white person would be shot or his store or other property destroyed by fire, in another part of the county. It became a regular thing, and the whites got as worried over the situation as they had made the Negroes. And then, one moonlight night, while Col. McClelland and his daughter and her suitor were sitting on his veranda, a party of men came in front of them, under the shade trees, and opened a deadly fire on them. The Colonel was maimed for life and his daughter and her suitor slain. That is my remembrance of it.[35]

Horror enveloped the white people. Their leaders went to Mr. Fortune and pleaded that a stop be put to such outrages, but he made the reply they had made to him, and with as much truth, that he did not know the authors of the outrages but he adventured the suggestion that if the whites would put a stop to their outrages on Negroes and carpet baggers he was of the opinion that the outrages on them would stop. And outrages in Jackson county eased up and tapered off, until a time came when there was no more of them. Unto this day it is not known who started the Negroes to retaliate in kind on the whites, any more than who the white leader was. But when black fire met white fire, both flaring in the dark, with death and conflagration for tool, the aggressors did not relish it. They never do.

The lawless right to murder carries with it the lawless right to be murdered. [PT: "The former never takes kindly to the latter."][36]

[NJG: September 10, 1927—
A Boy's Life in Reconstruction Days—Part Nine]
[PT: September 15, 1927—
Timothy Gets Into Trouble]

Boys will be boys. It is one of the endowments of childhood that never changes from sire to son. It makes of childhood and youth a stage of existence which is never lived over by the same person except in the transmission, and there is no other stage of life just like it or which the youngster remembers so long and affectionately as he journeys on the serpentine way from the cradle to the grave.

Timothy naturally wandered into the office of the Marianna Courier and picked up the first principles of a printer, which he was never to be master, but which served him a very helpful purpose as a breadwinner and in shaping his life for the work he was to do.[37] He had a natural liking for printing offices and never got over it. Indeed, much of such indifferent education as he was to receive was got in printing offices before he was of voting age. And the old printing offices were wonderful schools. In them Horace Greeley and Frederick Douglass learned much more than in the schools, which were few and poorly equipped in their day and were inaccessible, at least to Mr. Douglass, who simply picked up such education as he should need in after life as he went along and as a matter of course.[38] Mr. Lincoln was educated in much the same way. And what other Americans made a more valuable contribution to the history of their times than Greeley, Douglass and Lincoln? Timothy absorbed education naturally as he mastered the principles of typography, with the systematic reading and study which the work of a printer made necessary. Nature has a way of providing the sort of education a person needs, and usually starts him off in the way he should go and holds him to it.

Timothy had a weakness for marble playing. It was a craze with him. His parents could not trust him to go to town and return on time, especially on Saturdays, when the up-country boys came to town loaded with marbles which the town boys were anxious to win. In order to curb the weakness his parents took all the marbles from Timothy when he was to go to the village

Chipola River, Jackson County, FL. Photograph by Daniel R. Weinfeld.

on an errand, but Timothy managed to overcome this handicap by planting a certain number of marbles at a convenient point.

There was a bully in the village about eighteen who was as tough as steel. He did not look to be more than twelve, but he was built all in a heap and as strong as a young bull. He made it a business to cheat the youngsters and bluff himself out of trouble, or trounce the boy who accused him of cheating. On one occasion he was in the game and cheated and Timothy would not stand for it. He jumped on Timothy and the latter closed with him and grabbed him around his big neck dragged him to the ground and, while holding him beat him up. One of the boys ran to Timothy's father's shop, near by, and told him Joe Smith had Timothy down and was killing him. Emanuel Fortune came on the run with his shoe strap in his hand, and fell upon Joe and gave him a terrible drubbing, commanding him to let Timothy up, but Timothy had Joseph's legs and arms so tied up that he could not get up, and was getting a sound beating from above and below. His big brother came along and interfered; other joined in the scrap, and soon a small riot was in progress, which it took some time and much trouble to quell. Timothy still remained down, however, holding fast to Joseph and beating him up, until the unfortunate bully and he were literally pried apart. Timothy had no more trouble with Joseph after that scrap.

[NJG: "Timothy Encounters Vicious Day"]

One Saturday morning Emanuel Fortune was sick and wanted some whiskey. He sent Timothy to the village after it, with instructions to make haste quickly. Timothy did, until he ran into a bunch of up-country youngsters with plenty of marbles, and then he forgot all about his errand. Late in the afternoon, when it began to get dark, he remembered and hastened to get the liquor. Striking a lively trot warranted to last he started for home. When he came to the church yard, which the Yankee soldiers had laid waste, burning the fine church, a big dog with a heavy chain about his neck on the inside of the fence began to chase Timothy.[39] Timothy thought it was the devil broke loose and burned up the wind, and outdistanced the dog, chained about the neck as he was.

When he had run out of danger Timothy sat down to get his breath. He did more; he sampled the liquor and found that it was very good. He drank it gleefully, all there was in the big neck and felt very good but dizzy. When he reached home supper was being served and he took his place and did unusual justice to the repast. No questions had been asked him, but when the meal was finished the head of the house said: "Now, Timothy, I will attend to you." He did. When Timothy's mother thought he had been punished enough—he was the favorite child,—she said as much, and when her remonstrance went unheeded she grabbed a chair and went after the head of the house with blood in her eyes, insofar that he left off flogging Timothy and strove to defend himself by mollifying his irate wife. While he was doing this Timothy slipped out of the door and went under the house, where he had spent much of his spare time hunting noodles. The neighbors were aroused and a search for Timothy covered the big cornfield, with pine torches to light it, but it was far into the morning before Timothy crawled out from under the house and the search was called off and the wayward son hustled to bed, still whimpering from the smarting of the flogging, but forgiven for going up against the parental wrath.

[NJG: September 17, 1927—
A Boy's Life in Reconstruction Days—Part X]
[PT: September 22, 1927]

The Unwelcome Guest

When Timothy was twelve years old he felt his years. He always preferred the association of boys older than himself, and he so managed the tasks he had to perform in order to have freedom to enjoy himself as boys delight in, as to engage the co-operation of the older boys, who did most of the work while he over looked it. There is lots of fun in standing by and directing the work while others toil at it. In this way Timothy managed to get hauled enough wood in his little wagon to keep the fires going and to get the big yard swept over every Friday. These tasks had to be performed, and Timothy went about them in a business-like way, doing as little of the drudgery as he could not shove off on his big playmates, who appeared always willing and pleased to lend a hand. They made the work appear to be play, and that is what it amounted to. When gone about in this spirit work is always an easy and pleasant way to get rid of time and get the most out of living. It is when work is forced upon one, as an obligation or service, that it becomes irksome and distasteful. This is as true in the case of grown-ups as of youngsters.

Nearly every Saturday Timothy accompanied the senior Fortune on a fishing and hunting trip. The hunting part was incidental. The main business was to get enough fish for Sunday morning, and if any game got in the way to fetch it down. The fishing was mighty good and it was no great trouble to have a big catch as the result of the day's outing. The senior Fortune spent most of his time angling for big fish,—trout, white channel cat, and the like,—while Timothy angled industriously for black perch in the hollow of cypress trees bordering the streams, and which swarmed with good sized perch. The senior had a lot of fun angling for the big fellows, but Timothy caught the fish that made the Sunday breakfast a notable feast.

Emanuel Fortune had fitted out a barge and loaded it with poultry and garden produce and "poled it" to Apalachicola, an unheard of achievement, where he exchanged his products for flour, coffee and sugar, and some "goodies," none of which the people of Marianna had seen or tasted since before the civil war.[40] Corn meal, substitutes for coffee and brown sugar made at home had been the staples, and remained such for a long time, with plenty of home cured meats, milk and butter, and vegetables, all grown on "the place," as the phrase for the home acres was generally termed. And there was plenty to eat, after its kind. There wasn't any high cost of living to worry about because everybody raised his own supplies. They are fortunate who are in a position to do that and do it.

It was a memorable Sunday morning, when those first biscuits some of us had ever eaten were to be served. There was also the usual supply of fresh water fish and fried chicken. Uncle Joe Rolax, a good friend of the senior, had been invited to the breakfast. The children were not allowed at the table

Emanuel Fortune Jr. *Cleveland Gazette*, March 22, 1890. Ohio Historical Society.

with the grown-ups, of course. Excitement among them ran high. The feast was something they had looked forward to with the most abounding interest. They were going to have flour bread. There were no stoves in Marianna in those days. The open fireplace prevailed and the cooking was done in pots, ovens, and pans, with lids, with fire of hot coals above and beneath.

Mother Sarah Jane cooked many "bakings" of biscuits, and there seemed plenty and to spare. The children stood outside the kitchen door as the breakfast progressed and watched with great concern the gradual reduction in the biscuit supply. It appears that Uncle Rolax had an abnormal appetite for biscuit, which, added to the normal appetite of the other grown-ups, steadily devoured the biscuit supply.[41]

When no more than two helpings remained the children lost heart and began a loud wailing outside the kitchen door. They had become disconsolate and panicky over their disappointment. We all know how children feel when disappointed in matters of eating, as most of us have been children, although many are born old and never grow young. The children wailed so loudly and dolefully that the grown-ups rushed out to learn what the matter might be.

"What ails you uns?" screamed the mother, grabbing Timothy by the shoulders.

"Uncle Rolax is eating all th' biscuits!" he blubbered.

The astonishing answer broke up the breakfast feast, as far as the grown-ups were concerned, and saved to the children the small remainder of the biscuits. There was loud talk when the unwelcomed guest had departed of giving Timothy and the others a good thrashing for their conduct, but it ended in talk and many solemn warnings of what would happen if they ever did the like again.

It is quite wonderful what appetites some grown-ups have for certain things they like above others, and of which they appear never to get enough. A long time after war times I knew a distinguished race educator and diplomat, the first Afro-American Minister Resident and Consul General to Haiti, Hon. Ebenezer Don Carlos Bassett, who would eat a dozen big clams and more at one "standing," as we used to have the dealer open them at his Fulton Market place, and eat them [NJG: "from the shell as he opened them,"] while Dr. Booker T. Washington had a weakness for corn on the cob and would eat a half dozen ears at some of the daily luncheons we had together.[42]

[NJG: September 24, 1927—A Boy's Life in Reconstruction Days—Part XI]
[PT: September 29, 1927]

Klansman and Tiger Cat

One of the tasks young Timothy took pleasure in was herding the cattle in the late afternoon and rounding up the calves in the early morning. The calves seldom roamed far from home but the cattle often strayed miles away hunting new and better grazing. If they had gone so far that the bell the leader wore could not be heard, Timothy would mount a fine pony he owned and go in the general direction the herd had headed for in leaving the pen in the morning. Rounding up the cows was rare sport for the youngster and some times proved very exciting, especially when his cattle got mixed up with some other herd and had to be separated. Cattle are much like some people when they make up their minds and refuse to unmake it; they become stupidly stubborn. Master the bell cow, the leader, and the herd generally can be controlled. Timothy found it to be so, and I found it to be that way in after years in dealing with a lot of men in all sorts of gatherings.

Early one morning Timothy was out getting the calves started for the pen when he came upon a man sitting on a log fast asleep, with a rifle across his knees. Timothy came upon him suddenly and he was as startled as the sleeper, who jumped up and glared daggers at the boy, who refused to be worried in the least, however. It turned out to be Sergeant Barnes, the leader of the klansmen, who had been keeping watch for a chance to shoot the

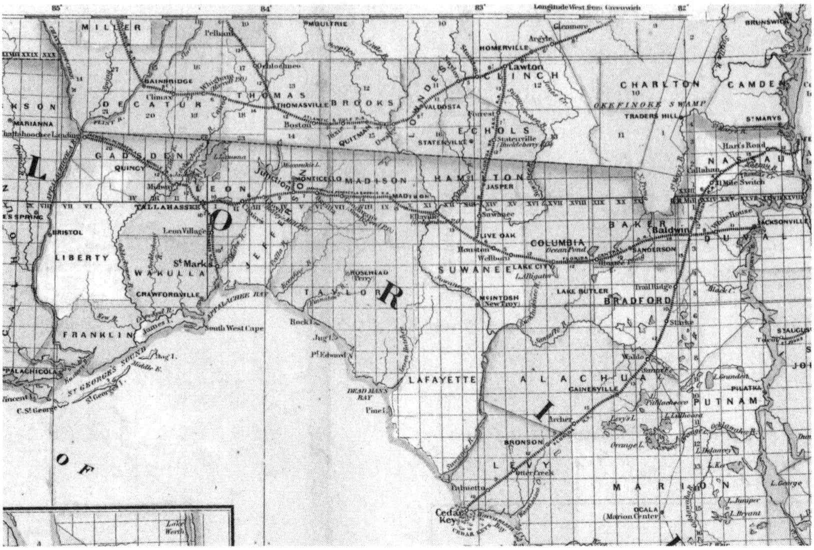

T. Thomas Fortune's Florida. Map by Asher & Adams (1871). Courtesy of Special and Digital Collections, Tampa Library, University of South Florida.

elder Fortune all night. And that was a nightly occurrence. Some one of them was on watch all the time after dark. On that account Emanuel Fortune, who had served his first session in the legislature, after serving in the constitutional convention, seldom remained in the village after sunset or left his house after nightfall. And he was always armed to the minute. Sergeant Barnes, after glaring at Timothy, stalked away towards the country district and away from the town and was soon hidden by the forest growth.[43]

Timothy was so absorbed thinking about the strange man with the rifle across his knees, and his villainous look—a long, lithe sharpshooter with an unblinking eye—that he quite forgot about the calves and where he was. He was lost in deep thought. As he emerged from a clump of scrub oak into a small open space he was more startled than when he came upon the armed sentinel to come face to face with an enormous tiger cat, known as a catamount by the country folks, a very ferocious beast, which gave the farmers much concern by destroying the young cattle. Timothy was more startled than afraid. The tiger cat appeared to be in the same way, as he held his head high and wagged his long tail, showing no disposition to run. Timothy continued to move towards the beast and was very near him when he turned and moved slowly in the direction Sergeant Barnes had taken.

When Timothy at last came to the calves and started them for the pen he was rather unnerved by the two meetings. He was disposed to get frightened after the danger had passed. This phase of his character grew pronounced as he grew in years, as he would get into and out of the most dangerous mix-ups and think nothing of the danger until it was all over.

The detachment of troops had long been disbanded and the soldier teachers had gone away and the little school was closed. It was all very sad for the Afro-American children, who took to school as ducks take to water. Major William J. Purman had been elected to the State Senate from Jackson county and Colonel Charles M. Hamilton had been elected to Congress, Florida at that time being entitled to only one member of the House of Representatives. Outrages grew, and prominent Negroes and carpet-baggers, as the Yankees were styled, lived in hourly danger of their lives and property.[44]

There was but one loyalist white family in the town—the Finlayson family, in which there were two sons and two daughters.[45] Dr. Finlayson and Major Purman became fast friends. One night about midnight the two friends were crossing an empty lot, going to the Major's lodging place, when a sharpshooter, standing beneath a spread oak a hundred yards away, the moon shining as brightly as the sun if possible, aimed to kill the Major, who was a head taller than the doctor, by shooting over the latter's head, but the bullet went through the doctor's temple and then lodged in the Major's neck. The doctor died instantly but the Major lived many years after, and succeeded Col. Hamilton in Congress.[46]

The assassination created the wildest excitement and carried dismay to the Negro people and all of the friends among the whites. The situation became so uncertain and dangerous that his white friends, and he had some good ones, advised Emanuel Fortune, because of his family, to move away, and he began to prepare to do so.[47]

[NJG: October 1, 1927—A Boy's Life in Reconstruction Days—Part XII]
[PT: October 6, 1927]

Leaving the Old Home

If you have never had to make preparations to leave the old home and relatives and friends of a life time, hope that you may not have to do so. It is more painful to be compelled by circumstances to do so than freely to do so to better your condition; but in either case the pain of going away cannot be shaken off. There is no place like home, however humble, it may be, as the good poet, who had no home himself, has told us in deathless song, and there never will be.

There was more than a mere matter of sentiment in the command of the Patriarch Abraham that he be buried, not in a strange land, but in the burying ground he had purchased in the Land of Canaan, where he had buried Sarah his wife, and Joseph directed that he be buried at Bethlehem, near his mother Rachel, and not among the strangers in Egypt, although, as in the case of Moses, he had been greatly honored and beloved by the Egyptians. But neither of them felt that Egypt was his home and desired that his body should sleep in the earth which the Lord had promised their fathers.

There is no condition one can live in which strains the nerves and confuses thought more than a lawless one; a condition in which a person knows that his life is at the mercy of any assassin who can catch him off his guard, and when he knows that his property may be destroyed while he sleeps. The Negroes of the South lived in that sort of condition all through the Reconstruction period, when none could call his life his own, and fear and demoralization dominated the lives of them all. The bulk of the whites lived in a state of confusion and uncertainty because they were equally ignorant of what would happen next. The farmer and merchant suffered alike with the working people in the crippled consumption which goes with crippled production. And this is always the case where lawlessness prevails and law and legal process are suspended or overridden.

Emanuel Fortune was not afraid of any man or combination of men, but the bravest hesitates when the enemy lurks in the dark or the brush with a rifle in one hand and a torch in the other. The American pioneers felt that way in their long conflict to wrest the land from the brave and undaunted Indian, who died to the last fighting to hold his own. Every Negro and Southern loyalist and carpet-bagger in Jackson county lived in constant fear of assassination.

When his white friends advised Emanuel Fortune to move to another part of the State he stoutly refused to consider the advice, but after the assassination of Dr. Finlayson and the wounding of Major Purman he changed his mind. He had five children and a frail wife, who was gradually dying under the fearful strain of expecting the death of her husband or the burning of her home, and he was persuaded that his duty to his helpless family, which such white friends as Joseph W. Russ, Edward Merritt, Major Purman, Colonel Hamilton and others, ceased not to advise him, required that he follow their good advice. He had gathered together some property, with

Florida's capitol, Tallahassee, 1870s. Courtesy of the State Archives of Florida.

much cattle and stock, but he could dispose of little of it because the people had no money, everybody being broke for a long season after war times, greenbacks getting into circulation in displacement of the Confederate paper money very slowly. He could not sell much, so he distributed it among his relatives and neighbors, with "promise to pay him when they could," and they never could.

When he went away to attend the second session of the legislature he took his little family with him, locating it at Jacksonville, with the exception of Timothy who was left at Tallahassee. When the legislature opened its session Timothy was elected one of the four page boys.[48] A larger life for the boy was thus opened for him. He received $3 per day in State script, which was discounted at 25 and 30 per cent, but Timothy never saw any of his pay. Emanuel Fortune received that, and needed it, as moving away from the old home left him poor indeed. But Timothy became very popular with the Senators by making himself useful in all possible ways; especially with the Democratic members, who were substantial professional and business men and farmers, who had plenty of ready cash, saving their salary in State script with which to pay their taxes. The Negro members and carpet-baggers had no cash and had to sell their script for what they could get.

Timothy had plenty of spending money all of the time. He built up the business of looking after the boots and shoes of the Senators and rendering any service required after the adjournment of the session for the day, and they paid him liberally for his time and service. The legislature was a very remarkable one as we shall find in the next two parts of "After War Times."

At this time life looked very bright and inviting to young Timothy.

[NJG: October 8, 1927—
A Boy's Life in Reconstruction Days—Part XIII]
[PT: October 13, 1927]

Page Boy Days

It is quite remarkable with what facility youth throws off the old and takes on the new in the passing show. Timothy was so captivated by the new scenes and faces his translation from a country town to the capital city of the State, although the city was nothing to brag about, having plenty of room to grow or shrink in, as the case might be, that he gave little thought to Marianna and its associations. He had his regrets, but the regrets of youth are very vague not grotesque or fantastic. He just appeared to fit in the new order and to take the unusual and unexpected as matters of course, adapting himself to them without apparent effort and in easy forgetfulness of the old life, short and turbulent as it had been in Marianna.[49]

It was considered a big thing among the young folks of both races to be a page boy in the Florida legislature. Among the youngsters it was as big a thing as being a member of the legislature. Timothy became a marked boy and took his place as a leader among the youngsters of his race in all of their activities. He took his place in the Sunday-school, of course, and thus became by that token a member of the best society of youngsters in Tallahassee. Mr William Steward, cashier of the Freedmen's bank branch at Tallahassee, was superintendent. He was a very superior man. His brother, Rev. Theophilus G. Steward, died recently at Wilberforce University, a retired Chaplain of the United States army, with the rank of Major. Mr. William Steward is still living at Bridgeton, N. J. He belongs to the Gouldtown people, a settlement of race people in Jersey which has contributed many distinguished men and women to the service of the race in its church and school work.[50]

The young set at Tallahassee was made up of some fine boys and girls, some of whom made a big mark in the world. Timothy's immediate associate

Thomas V. Gibbs. Courtesy of the State Archives of Florida.

was Thomas V. Gibbs, whose father, Rev. Jonathan C. Gibbs, was at that time secretary of State, and subsequently was appointed by Governor Harrison Reed as State Secretary of Education, in which office he died. He was a graduate of Amherst, if I remember correctly, and an able clergyman of the Presbyterian Church, leaving a Philadelphia church to serve in Florida. His son Thomas Victor was a very extraordinary young man. He attended Oberlin College and was appointed a cadet to West Point military academy but was not allowed to get by the color bar. His father died while he was yet at college and he had to give up the ambition to secure a university education. It was a great disappointment. He became an educator and at the time of his death was assistant principal of the State Normal school at Tallahassee. He has a son who is a successful physician, with an interesting family, at Trenton, N. J. His uncle was the wellknown Judge Mifflin W. Gibbs of Arkansas, who played a very conspicuous part in the Reconstruction politics and business life of the race in that State after war times.[51]

Besides Thomas V. Gibbs the immediate associates of Timothy were three young men with social standing and aspirations, and the four of them set the social pace. The elders in the legislature had no more social life of it, and they had plenty, than the young folks of the city.

During this time there came to Tallahassee a young man of the name Napier, a brother of our James C. Napier, the successful lawyer and banker and civic worker of Nashville, who married the only daughter of Hon. John Mercer Langston, who created among other things, the law department of Howard University, of which he was acting President after the retirement of General Oliver O. Howard, and was acting as such when Timothy entered Howard in 1874. Mr Langston served eight years as Minister Resident and Counsel General to Haiti. He was a fine scholar, a notable educator, and one of the best orators the race has produced. He also served a term in Congress from Virginia and wrote a notable story of his life. Mr. Langston thought himself to be a greater man than Frederick Douglass, but he just happened not to be. The rivalry between the two kept Washington society on tip toe for many years, and was very amusing in some of its phases, as Mr. Douglass was as modestly retiring as Mr. Langston was aggressively haughty and assertive.[52]

Young Napier came upon the young race folks of Tallahassee as a revelation. He had failed to get through the West Point color bar, as young Gibbs had. He was young, good looking, and he "dressed to kill." The young race folks just thought he was it, the likes of which they had never seen before. But he did not remain upon the scene for long. He came in a flash and left in a flash, but the remembrance of his apparent brilliance made a lasting impression upon the young folks of Tallahassee.[53]

*[NJG: October 15, 1927—
A Boy's Life in Reconstruction Days—Part XIV]
[PT: October 20, 1927—"Timothy Hit It Right"]*

There were some very interesting race characters in the legislature of Florida in the Reconstruction days. Many of them were very intelligent and enjoyed a fair degree of education, and most of them were orators, as the term is generally understood. They could talk at length and with some show of information on any subject proposed in the legislature. The race still has a great many talkers of the word. There are many doers also, it is fair to grant, but they are fewer than the talkers, although they get the better and more appreciable results, and are regarded as the more substantial and dependable citizens. The gift of gab is a wonderful one, and it may turn out finally to be a blessing that the Negro race possesses so large a part in the gift.

Among the senators our ministers were the most numerous. Rev. Charles

H. Pierce of Leon, Rev. Robert Meacham of Jefferson, and Rev. Charles L. Bradwell of Duval counties were conspicuous. They measured up to the mental stature of the average white "cracker" senators, who were none too intelligent and none too eloquent, but were solid citizens all the same, being fruit growers and professional men for the most part, with plenty of cash money to spend without dependence upon the salary paid in depreciated state script for their services. In the Assembly, Emanuel Fortune of Jackson, Frederick Hill of Gadsden, A. B. Osgood of Madison, Rev. John R. Scott of Duval and Harry S. Harmon of Alachua counties, were outstanding characters, intelligent and shrewd, with wide-open eyes to the main chance, which was not always reached by the straight and narrow path, and much crooked business went on which helped to bring the Reconstruction government into disrepute and ultimate downfall.[54]

General Butler of Walton county was one of the extraordinary characters among the carpet baggers. He was not a brainy or cultured man but he had plenty of horse sense and was built on swagger lines. He was very bulky, with a Teuton face and a fierce mustache that stood out like that of President Von Hindenburg of Germany, who proved to be just a little less great in war than General Foch of the French, and who has saved Germany to be a great Republic in peace. General Butler of Walton was the only white Republican in his county, and held all of the lucrative offices—county clerk, and the like—and had piles of cash greenbacks on him all the time. He was the admitted Croesus of the legislature.[55]

General Butler had an intelligent Negro understudy named Valentine, who was a very amiable and shrewd member. Like his master he had always plenty of cash in hand. He boarded at the same place as Timothy and a good understanding grew up between them. There was a great deal of hard drinking among the Republican legislators and hangers on, and Otis' saloon seldom closed until the small hours of the morning. Bedlam usually reigned in the place, but there was never anything doing which bordered on the disorderly. They were just having a high old time among themselves. It is quite marvelous how low a high old time will drag those who pursue the phantom long enough.

One afternoon Timothy discovered that Mr. Valentine was not only drinking heavily but that he had a big bundle of money about him. After dinner, which was usually late in the afternoon, Mr. Valentine and other members resorted as usual to Otis'. Timothy began to think about the money Mr. Valentine had on him and grew fearful that he might lose it

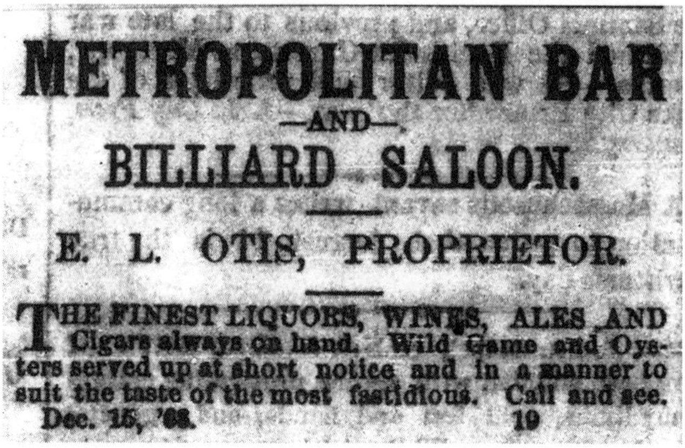

Otis's saloon advertisement, *Tallahassee Weekly Floridian*, January 1869. Courtesy of the State Archives of Florida.

while drinking. About nine o'clock Timothy squeezed into the place and found Mr. Valentine and the others going the pace that kills.

Mr. Valentine recognized Timothy when the latter tugged at his coat sleeves and, separating from the others, asked as coherently as he could what he wanted. Timothy told him he had better let him take and keep his money for him until the morning. The idea appealed to him and he readily gave Timothy the big roll of money. Timothy got out of the place in a jiffy and made for his boarding place. He tried to count the money but never was able to get further than $900, although there was some more. He was so overcome with the responsibility of having the money that he was unable to sleep at all, and was wide awake at breakfast time. So was Mr. Valentine, but he had the most woebegone expression on his face I ever saw. He was utterly cast down and got all of his friends guessing, as he was the jolly member of the group, but he would not explain.

When others had gone to the capital, Mr. Valentine remained behind. Timothy then approached and asked him what the trouble was. He said he had lost all his money, some $1500, and did not know how he did it. Timothy held him in suspense for a while and then asked him if he did not remember giving him the roll of bills at Otis', but he shook his head and said he did not remember anything about it. Timothy then handed over the roll to him. I have never seen a happier man since. He asked Timothy what he wanted most and Timothy instantly answered that he wanted a pair of

Stanton Institute, Jacksonville, Florida, 1880s. Courtesy of the State Archives of Florida.

boots, boots then being the thing with men and youngsters. Mr. Valentine told Timothy he should have the boots and all that goes with them. He took him to the best store in the city and selected the finest boots for boys in it; then he selected a fine hat, and then a complete new suit of fine clothes. Oh Joy! Timothy has never felt again the satisfaction he had when he dressed in the new things and showed up in the Senate as the best dressed page boy of his times.

[NJG: October 22, 1927—A Boy's Life in Reconstruction Days—Part XV]
[PT: October 27, 1927]

Death of the Mother

Timothy developed very rapidly in the new atmosphere. Mingling with young people older and more advanced in the rudiments of education than he, rubbing elbows with legislators, and spending much of his spare time in the office of the *Sentinel,* whose owner, Mr. Walton, a Northern man, was the State Printer and had taken a fancy to Timothy, "sticking type," with the Sunday school and plenty of social life among the young people, many of the girls of which were very pretty and quite superior in many ways. Timothy expanded rapidly and began to use his eyes and understanding for what they were given him, to weigh men and measures at their proper value. On the whole, the Afro-American members of the legislature were a capable lot, averaging in intelligence their native white and carpet bag associates.[56]

Timothy Serves as Private Secretary

Little Pons of Escambia county was the freak member, being little larger than Tom Thumb; Harry S. Harmon of Alachua county was the dandy, the lady's man, very intelligent and alert, and a very ready speaker; General Josiah T. Walls, a former Union soldier, was Adjutant-General of Militia and every inch a soldier, and carried his sword as a soldier to buttress the dignity of his position, which was greatly enlarged when he became Congressman a few years later, Timothy serving him as private secretary after he reached Washington, in 1873; Emanuel Fortune of Jackson county was the sober-sided plodder, a ready speaker and persuasive, who got himself in bad by opposing the tendency to extravagance and high handed methods which the white carpet-baggers adopted as a policy for their selfish purposes and which helped to bring about the overthrow of the Reconstruction government of the State.[57]

The Republicans gave Florida a splendid constitution, under which it is still working without amendment, and a public school system, the foundations of which were laid by Dr. Jonathan C. Gibbs, concerning whom I have already spoken, which was sufficient for the needs of the people; but it also went in for extravagant expenditures of public moneys, necessitating a very high rate of taxation, and for voting away rich franchises without adequate safeguarding of the public interests, railway rights of way being among them.[58]

The session was drawing to a close. Timothy took a week end off to see his mother at Jacksonville, as she was sick unto death from work and worry, which the brief years of freedom appeared to multiply for her, who was born to years of slavery and insult and enforced labor, which eat up frail, sensitive creatures as the canker and the worm devour the things they hitch themselves upon. And she was high strung and sensitive, small of stature and beautiful of figure and features, unfitted in every way for the hard life which became her portion as the mother of five children at the age of thirty-six years. The wherefore of it must remain a mystery, a thing of horror to abhor and anathematize, as embodied in the slave system and the brutalities of the Ku Klux Klan, of which she was a victim.

Timothy spent three days with his sick mother in Jacksonville and returned to the capital, hopeful that she was improving in health. How easy is it to see the way you hope! But the Monday morning session of the legislature had hardly got going before Timothy got a telegram saying that his mother was dead. The light appeared to go out of his young life, and everything became magnified that his eyes rested upon. He hastened to catch the afternoon train. He was such a favorite that, among others, the railroad officials would give him all the transportation for which he asked, insofar that up to the time he left for Washington, Timothy never had to pay a cent for transportation in Florida.[59]

Timothy Moves From Slave Boy to Newspaper Editor

Timothy walked through the sandy city, with plank walks only here and there, as one in a daze. Everything seemed magnified and strange. The boy died with the mother, and looking back over the long past, I much doubt if Timothy ever recovered a normal life. His wonderful precocity and adaptability to every situation seemed uncanny to others and as a dream to him, who was led as it were from an ignorant boy without scholastic training, out of a slave condition, to hold many high positions in the Federal service and to become editor of a powerful newspaper and the organizer of great race civic organizations before he was twenty-five years of age. But such was his strange destiny.

Timothy reached the humble home where his young mother lay dead, but the light had gone out of him and he remembered nothing, from the time he entered the house until he found himself back in Tallahassee a few days after. She loved him as he loved her with an unearthly feeling which we strive in vain to analyze and understand. A few days before she was alive and taking Timothy by the hand had said that if anything happened to her he should always look after and care for the young children. Now she was dead and gone away in the shadows, where she could not be seen or heard any more by him who loved her as he loved himself. And the four young children, all younger than Timothy, could not realize what the Lord had done for them in taking the mother and leaving them more than bereft,—desolate and helpless in the cold hands of the heartless world.[60]

The legislative session closed and Timothy went to Jacksonville, but he was not the same Timothy who had left Marianna two years before. Tragedy had come into his life and blasted his childhood, leaving him a child in years to face the trials and tribulations of a man,—a radical change which he came but slowly to realize and to grasp as best he could.

[PT: "Life is a desperate game which the wisest man fights with the cards stacked against him without his knowing it. He is only and simply a medium."]

[NJG: October 29 1927—A Boy's Life in Reconstruction Days—Part 16] *[PT: November 3, 1927—Death of the Mother]*

Looking back over it, I am sure the reader will agree with me, that it was no small matter for young Timothy, just over the legal age of sixteen years to receive an appointment to be a mail route agent from the Postmaster-General at Washington. It came about quite in the usual way, however. Timothy was a favorite of Congressman William J. Purman, who came up in the Marianna and Tallahassee days with Emanuel Fortune as his political associate and friend. Joseph Raines of Monticello, a very capable young man of the race, was serving as mail route agent on the J. P. & M. Railroad, when his car left the tracks above Monticello Junction and he was crushed to death. Timothy left Jacksonville on his trial trip in the shadow of this tragedy.[61]

The railroad bed and tracks had been allowed to run down to the worst condition, the ties being defective as the rails. The East Florida soil is very sandy and in wet weather it was necessary to run the trains at a low rate of speed to prevent them from jumping the tracks. As it was it was rough going, with accidents always possible at any time.

Timothy Makes Rapid Assortment of Mails

On the return trip to Jacksonville from Chattahoochee, as far as the road then reached, the change of cars had been made at Live Oak to the heavy train of the Atlantic and Gulf road from Savannah, and the big car was piled high with mail.[62] Timothy was making rapid assortment of it. It was rather coolish, and early in the morning. The stove was roaring hot with pine knots. Timothy went to one of the doors on the right side, and slid it back, after leaving Sanderson, then pulled it to and chained it. This saved his life. As the train moved up grade to the Olustee tressle, and fifty yards from the woodwork, the big mail car turned over on its side and slid down the steep embankment. Timothy fell forward into the door he had chained and was only stunned. Frank Eppes, the fireman, crawled on top of the car and broke a window in the side, and in answer to the clamor of the onlookers, Timothy sat up in the door and answered:

"No, I ain't dead."

Great Rejoicing Among Passengers

There was a great rejoicing among passengers and crew. Timothy gathered up his big mail, which was scattered and littered everywhere, and we proceeded to Jacksonville in a freight car. There was no certainty when we should go it again and Timothy went home and to bed as fast as he could. About 2 o'clock he was notified to report at once, and we started on the out-trip with the mail in a freight car. Soon after leaving Baldwin, the first station out, the freight car jumped the track and straddled it without turning over, Timothy got a bad shake up and a bad fright and much jumbled mail, and he did some tall thinking about his new job and whether he wanted to keep it. The two accidents in the same trip made him think rapidly. He decided that he liked the big job and would stick to it. After awhile the train moved on towards Chattahoochee and there were no more mishaps of that kind. It took two nights and a day to make the round trip. We had to sleep in the coaches at Chattahoochee as there were no houses there, and we had to keep the coaches sealed tight as the mosquitoes, bred in the swamp were the most numerous, able-bodied and ferocious I ever knew before or since.

All Afro-American Agents in Florida

All the agents in Florida were Afro-Americans, three on the J. P. & M. and three on the Florida railroads. On my run were B. F. Cox, one of the finest young men I ever knew, and A. B. Osgood, a real gentleman. There was a special agent with headquarters at Atlanta who had a big prejudice against Afro-American agents, and he did all he could to annoy them and get them into trouble; so they all combined to give him trouble, aided by "Old Man"

Dale of the A. & G. road, one of the best white men I ever knew, and who enjoyed the confidence of C. J. French, the District Superintendent at Chattanooga. Each trip we all had a complaint to lodge against Walker.[63]

Some Example of Him And His Ways

Here are some examples of him and his ways. He dropped a letter, unsealed in my car box at Live Oak, addressed to a party at Lake City, three stations beyond. I looked into it and found a ten dollar bill in it. I made the mail messenger at Lake City sign for it and got a receipt for it from the postmaster. Another time, at Live Oak, just after we had transferred to the big A. & G. mail car, I was standing at the door looking on, with the chain up, when Walker swung on the steps, they were high up—and began pulling himself up. I put my right foot under his chin and sent him sprawling. He jumped up fighting mad, exclaiming he was a special agent.

"You can't bolt into a mail car. It's against the rules. How do I know you are a special agent?" said Timothy, innocent place like. While they were disputing the train pulled out and Walker had to scramble for it to get into a regular day coach.

The Business of the Mail Agent

It was the business of the mail agent to verify and keep a record of the weighing of the mails for a certain number of days as taken by the railroad officials. The following morning, on reaching Jacksonville, Walker bolted into the weighing room and interfered with the weighing of the mail. I gave him to understand that that was my job and if he insisted on interfering I would leave it to him and so report. The railroad agent also objected and he had to step out, raving mad. Then he tried to get into the mail wagon to ride to the post-office but I objected and the driver whipped up the team and left him fuming at the station. [PT: "All these doings of Walker were promptly reported to Superintendent French, and coupled with the reports of other agents they had the effect of separating Walker from the service and the payroll of the government."]

[NJG: November 5, 1927—A Boy's Life in Reconstruction Days—Part 18]
[PT: November 10, 1927—Death of the Mother]

All the mail route agents in Florida and Georgia were glad to be rid of Special Agent Walker. It is wonderful how much trouble a man "clothed with

Customhouse and Post Office, Jacksonville, Florida, 1870s. Courtesy of the State Archives of Florida.

a little brief authority," can give those in subordinate places under him.

When Timothy had been in the service a month he received a registered letter chaser from the Department and he got anxious at once, as all mail agents do until they find that they have a proper receipt for the missing package. When he got the leisure on the way to Jacksonville, Timothy ran through his registration book hastily and was surprised not to find any entry of the package at all. It looked as if he had never received it. Time and again he went through the book with the same result. It looked black. If an agent could not show a receipt for a package traced to him he was promptly arrested by a United States marshal.

No Trace of the Package Found

Timothy fretted and fumed all the way to Jacksonville, but search after search did not show anywhere that he had received the package indicated by the tracer. When he reached the Jacksonville post office he called the matter to the attention of Felix A. Canover, a clerk with whom he had long worked, and a very fine white man, a sort of head of the clerical force. He went through the book carefully once or twice and could find no trace of the package. He was puzzled, as he never for a moment questioned Timothy's integrity, any more than I did. But here was the tracer and there was no record of it!

Timothy went to his home for refreshments and rest and felt way down in the mouth. He prided himself on his honesty and here he was as it seemed, face to face with the United States marshal with a warrant for his arrest. When he returned to the post office in the afternoon to go out on his run, Timothy had very little spirit left in him. He was limp with apprehension. Mr. Canover told him he had been thinking over the matter of the tracer ever since his attention had been called to it and that he had reached the conclusion that the missing package must be in the old unused portion of the registration book Timothy had to take on his first run out, as it was two weeks after he entered the service before his outfit came from Washington. The suggestion seemed to be a life saver to the young agent. The two of them went after that old book in a hurry and were soon poring over its entries. Their search bore immediate results. They soon came upon the entry of the missing package, with the signature of a Florida division agent after it. What a relief! Life at once appeared again to be worth while.

Young Man Arrested and Sent to Prison

The young man who had signed for the package was unable to show that he had delivered it to the next due to receive it, and he was arrested and tried and sentenced to serve time in a Federal prison. He was a fine specimen of a man of the race, but he could not deny himself the temptation of living beyond his means after becoming an agent and making more money than he had ever made before. He got into the "fast set" and ruined his life. Everybody was sorry for him, because he was popular and likable. He and the postal clerk who took Timothy's place in the post office when the latter had a row with the acting postmaster, were the only Afro-American employees who went wrong and were jailed during the Reconstruction days in Florida. Does it pay to be honest? Certainly, when not dealing with crooks.

[PT: "AN UGLY STATION AGENT"]

Laying over at Chattahoochee, as I have said, was a very disagreeable business, as there were no houses there, with the exception of the station agent's shack. Being single, he lived in a part of the shack and had a handy man to help with the freight and do his housework. He was a young man with a

513 **JACKSONVILLE, PENSACOLA AND MOBILE RAILROAD.**

R. Walker, Receiver and Gen. Superintendent.
H. L. Magee, Assistant Superintendent.

Jas. L. Taylor, Gen. Freight and Ticket Agent.
General Offices—Tallahassee, Fla.

TIME-SCHEDULE IN EFFECT MAY 17, 1874, AND UNTIL FURTHER NOTICE.

FROM CHATTAHOOCHEE RIVER TO JACKSONVILLE.

(*Savannah time.*)	Mls	Pass'ger.	Pass'ger.
Lve. **Chattahoochee Riv**[1]	0	6 20 A.M.	
" Chattahoochee	3	6 35 "	
" Mount Pleasant	11	7 25 "	
" Quincy	20	8 10 "	
" Midway	32	9 00 "	
Arr. **Tallahassee**	44	9 50 A.M.	
Lve. **St. Marks**[2]	0	12 55‡ P.M.	
Arr. **Tallahassee**	21	2 20 P.M.	
Lve. **Tallahassee**	44	*2 30 P.M.	
" Chaires'	56	3 20 "	
" Lloyd's	62	3 55 "	
Arr. **Junction**	71	4 45 P.M.	
Lve. **Junction**	71	4 50 P.M.	8 20 A.M.
Arr. **Monticello**	75	5 10 P.M.	8 40 A.M.
Lve. **Junction**	71	4 45 P.M.	
" Aucilla	78	5 25 "	
" Goodman's	85	6 05 "	
" Madison	99	7 00 "	
" Ellaville	114	8 00 "	
Arr. **Live Oak**[3]	127	9 00 P.M.	
Lve. **Savannah**	0	*4 30 P.M.	
Arr. **Live Oak**[3]	179	3 55 A.M.	
Lve. **Live Oak**[3]	127	*4 10 A.M.	
" Houston	133	4 35 "	
" Welborn	138	4 55 "	
" **Lake City** (Florida Central Railroad)	150	5 50 "	
" Olustee (Florida Central Railroad)	160	6 45 "	
" Sanderson (Florida Central Railroad)	172	7 30 "	
" Darbysville (Florida Central Railroad)	181	8 10 "	
" **Baldwin**[4] (Florida Central Railroad)	190	9 00 "	
" White House (Florida Central Railroad)	198	9 30 "	
Arr. **Jacksonville**[5] (Florida Central Railroad)	206	10 15 A.M.	

‡ Tuesday, Thursday and Saturday only. * Daily. Other trains daily, except Sunday.

FROM JACKSONVILLE TO CHATTAHOOCHEE RIVER.

(*Savannah time.*)	Mls	Pass'ger.	Pass'ger.
Lve. **Jacksonville**[5] (Florida Central Railroad)	0	*2 40 P.M.	
" White House (Florida Central Railroad)	11	3 30 "	
" **Baldwin**[4] (Florida Central Railroad)	19	4 10 "	
" Darbysville (Florida Central Railroad)	28	4 50 "	
" Sanderson (Florida Central Railroad)	37	5 30 "	
" Olustee (Florida Central Railroad)	47	6 15 "	
" **Lake City** (Florida Central Railroad)	59	7 10 "	
" Welborn	71	8 05 "	
" Houston	76	8 25 "	
Arr. **Live Oak**[3]	82	8 50 P.M.	
Lve. **Live Oak**[3]	82	*9 05 P.M.	
Arr. **Savannah**	261	8 20 A.M.	
Lve. **Live Oak**[3]	82	*4 10 A.M.	
" Ellaville	95	5 10 "	
" Madison	110	6 20 "	
" Goodman's	124	7 00 "	
" Aucilla	131	7 40 "	
Arr. **Junction**	138	8 15 A.M.	
Lve. **Monticello**	0	7 30 A.M.	4 00 P.M.
Arr. **Junction**	4	7 50 A.M.	4 20 P.M.
Lve. **Junction**	138	8 15 A.M.	
" Lloyd's	147	8 55 "	
" Chaires	153	9 25 "	
Arr. **Tallahassee**	165	10 15 A.M.	
Lve. **Tallahassee**	0	10 55‡ A.M.	
Arr. **St. Marks**[2]	21	11 50 A.M.	
Lve. **Tallahassee**	165	10 30 A.M.	
" Midway	177	11 20 A.M.	
" Quincy	189	12 10 P.M.	
" Mount Pleasant	198	12 55 "	
" Chattahoochee	206	1 45 "	
Arr. **Chattahoochee Riv**[1]	209	2 00 P.M.	

CONNECTIONS.—[1] With Central line of boats for Apalachicola, Eufaula, Columbus and all north-western points, via Montgomery and Eufaula R. R. to Montgomery. [2] With Gulf Steamers for Key West, Cedar Keys, Pensacola, New Orleans, &c. [3] With Atlantic and Gulf Railway, for Savannah, and points north and east, via Savannah and Jesup Junction. [4] With Florida Railroad for Fernandina, Gainesville, Cedar Keys, &c. [5] With Brock's celebrated Line of Steamers on the St. John's River, for Palatka, Tocoi, St. Augustine, &c., for particulars of which see special advertisement of those steamers.

Jacksonville, Pensacola and Mobile Railroad Map and Schedule, 1874. *Traveler's Official Guide of the Railway and Steam Navigation Lines in the United States and Canada*. Philadelphia, National Railway Publication Company, 1874.

fiery temper and was known to be quick with his pistol. He was the son of a former Confederate general, and as full of arrogance and insolence as an oyster is of meat. The station was five miles from the river and the agent met the boat from Chattahoochee and Columbus by hand car, which his handy man worked,—and a handcar requires some more work!

To while away the time, Timothy and the handy man used to go up or down the road a short ways to pick blackberries and loaf. They did not go far, and were always back in time to take the station agent to the boat. One day they went farther than usual and the boat reached the landing and was blowing lustily for the agent while they were yet some distance up the track. When they reached the station the agent was crazy with anger, and went after the handy man, who was very much afraid of him, like an unchained Fury.

Timothy knew General Dickinson very well, having come in contact with him in the Tallahassee days. He was a very amiable, affable and courteous gentleman of the old school. He also knew young Dickinson very well. And Timothy never came into contact with a white or black man he was afraid of. He promptly stepped between young Dickinson and the handy man, explaining that he and not the handy man was to blame and that he was very sorry the thing happened. Young Dickinson's wrath oozed out rapidly and he remarked that if that was the way of it he would overlook it, but he did not want it to happen again. And it did not. The chances are that if young Timothy had not stepped in young Dickinson would have given the handy man a good kicking as well as cussing. He had a reputation for doing that sort of thing and thought it was smart.[64]

And the old flat bottomed boat had to wait five miles away for the station agent, whom the handy man landed at the water edge in faster time than a hand car had ever before made on the J. P. & M. Railroad.

[NJG: November 12, 1927—A Boy's Life in Reconstruction Days—Part 19]
[PT: November 17, 1927]

The Summons to Washington

It is always a difficult and disagreeable business to have to start all over again in a strange place after you have succeeded in the old place among those you have always known. It is best to put up with a lot of hardship in the old place among those you have always known than to move away and have to build a new foundation in acquaintances and friendships and the opportunities that make for the necessary "crust of bread and a place to sleep." Emanuel Fortune found it to be so in moving from West to East Florida. He had but little money and the opposition of the ruling Republican machine and the Democratic people to contend with. Jacksonville had no municipal government at that time and old General Edward Hopkins and other Democratic veterans and dependable citizens soon came to like the new man from the West country.[65] They gave him encouragement and all the credit he needed to make ends meet, and he managed in his way to keep in close touch with his obligations, with the assistance of Timothy, who was adding a dollar to the family capital all the time. Indeed, Timothy was for some time the main breadwinner of the family and took great pride in so being. He made good money all of the time and handed over most of it to the head of the house.[66]

A charter had been secured and a city election was to be held. Emanuel Fortune, who had great respect and admiration for General Hopkins, prevailed upon the grand old Confederate who had so befriended him to be the independent candidate for Mayor. Mr. Fortune had an independent convention held and the General was nominated for mayor, and Mr. Fortune for city marshal, with a common council body. The Afro-Americans voted solidly for the independent candidates, while many of the whites voted for the ticket because they had confidence in General Hopkins, a gentleman of the old school,—long and gaunt and strong in the characteristics that make for leadership. The city government was organized along liberal and tolerant lines, with a development in the police and fire and other departments in which the Afro-Americans were equally represented with the whites. It made a very strong city government, which lasted two years, and was not overthrown for several years, and then only by taking away the city charter and substituting the commission government system, with appointments to be made by the Governor of the administrative officers. This was done to get rid of the Negro in control of the affairs of the city.[67]

But the Negro himself helped to destroy the independent party of his co-equal share in the conduct of municipal affairs by drawing the Republican party line and working hand in glove with such white carpet-baggers as objected to the leadership of Mr. Fortune, aided and abetted by Rev. John R. Scott, Rev. Joseph E. Lee, Rev. W. W. Sampson and others, who created a condition of confusion and rowdyism in election campaigns which disgusted good citizens with the Republican party and its riotous ways.[68]

Rev. Joseph E. Lee did the Negro of Jacksonville and Florida more injury than any other man. He was a graduate of the Institute for Colored Youth at Philadelphia and of the law department of Howard University. He was the most selfish and greedy Negro I ever knew. At one time he was a lawyer in practice, a justice of the peace, secretary of the Republican State and chairman of the county committee, Presiding elder of the Jacksonville district and pastor of Great Mt. Zion A. M. E. Church. He went into the Internal Revenue office as a clerk the first week he was in Jacksonville, and he ruled Florida Republican party politics for his own advantage until the time of his mysterious death in his office a few years ago.[69]

Mr. Lee's method was to control the Negro and to so work with the

Joseph E. Lee and A. M. E. Ministers. Courtesy of the State Archives of Florida.

white Republican leaders as to secure for himself the best Federal position in the State, regardless of the interests of others, so that when he died the Negro in Florida had been frozen out of the public service, with the exception of himself. He destroyed all of the good and honorable opportunities for public service which Mr. Fortune had made possible for the Negro in the State. He was the first Negro as I remember it who ever drew the color line, arraying blacks against the other race colors, to carry his point in a Negro convention. So he got what he wanted, others of the race could go hang, as the saying is. He was so thrifty that it was said he had soaked away the first dollar he made in Florida and was so stingy that he bought a home a few yards outside the city limits in order to escape paying city taxes. He was a shrewd man and thrifty, but it would have been well for the Negro of Florida if Joseph E. Lee had remained in his Philadelphia home instead of carpet-bagging it in Florida.

One day Timothy got a message from Congressman Purman requesting him to resign from the position of mail route agent and to report to him at Washington as he had a better job for him. The spoils system was the rule in those days. Everything went by favor of the Senator and member of Congress. Major Purman wanted to reward an old friend and party worker, and Timothy was asked to step up higher. "The new man was too old and too illiterate to do the work, and did not remain long in the service, but he had his reward."

Timothy liked the mail service and regretted to leave it, but he had high hopes of getting a college education, and it was with that thought uppermost that he prepared to leave for the capital of the Nation. He left Jacksonville with very little money and what came near developing into a dangerous riot. Conductor Livingstone refused to allow him to enter the first class coach, and the hundred of Negro draymen at the station threatened to do the conductor up. Timothy cancelled his ticket by rail and took the steamer for Charleston and from thence to Washington, and first class accommodations all the way. The color line in travel was just then being inaugurated in Florida and the South.

[NJG: November 19, 1927]
A Boy's Life in Reconstruction Days—Part 20

I would like to tell of some of the things that befell Timothy in Charleston and on the trip to Washington by the old broken down Washington and Weldon Railroad that has long since been merged into something better. The trip was full of interest and excitement, after its kind, opening as it did a new world for the youngster. When he got to Washington he went to the Philadelphia House on Pennsylvania avenue. It was kept by Col. Perry H. Carson, a stalwart Negro who in time came to be a great power in District and National politics as a National Committee man. His Blaine Invincible Republication organization became famous and a great power. Col. Carson was not an educated man, but he had plenty of common sense and he knew how to organize and lead the ignorant masses of his race. He was a great if not a saintly leader. He knew how to get the most out of the political spoils system, and had the government offices in the District of Columbia filled with his henchmen. All his offices holders paid tribute to Col. Carson, whose hotel and bar were a regular hangout of as tough a political aggregation as flourished anywhere else.[70]

Made Special Agent of the Treasury Department

It is easier for Congressman Purman to request Timothy to come up higher than to secure him an appointment in the Federal service. Everybody out of office was using his influence to get in, and a Florida Congressman did not have much of a pull. After many days, and when Timothy's bank roll had dwindled to the vanishing point, Mr. Purman secured Timothy a commission as special agent of the Treasury department for the District of Delaware at $3.50 per diem. Timothy went to Wilmington, not knowing anything about the customs service or its requirements, but he visited the custom house every day and did what was assigned him, with the disfavor of Collector Nolan and his son, the inspector, and his assistant, I. K. Jump, to contend with, as much on account of color as resentment at his being given a job they thought should have been given a native of the State.[71]

Timothy made his home with Mr. Jackson, janitor of the Federal building, who made it pleasant for him. He got into the social swim easily enough, with bright young people like the Misses Purnell, Graves, Williamsons, Browns, Edwina B. Cruse, who was then teaching at Middleton, but after became famous as principal of Howard School at Wilmington, and who is still living, with a lot of young men, who were real bright and promising. Life was very pleasant, in a social way for Timothy, and he was learning something new all of the time, being a diligent student of people and books and things. There was much of concert, theatre, picnic and social activities, going on most of the time, Timothy being the escort of two or three young women at most of these outings.[72]

Never Caught Any of the Smugglers

And when Timothy was sent to the Delaware Breakwater, at Lewes, where there was much smuggling, with Philadelphia as the headquarters, but Timothy never caught any of the smugglers, although he did his best to do so. He got in bad with the whites when he reached the town by registering at the little white hotel and remaining there two days and nights before the keeper found out he was "colored."[73] The whites were a very narrow and race prejudiced lot, but Timothy managed to make friends among them. A Mr. Knowles published the Breakwater Light, a weak, weekly, and he and his family welcomed Timothy to the family and the printing office. He got busy setting type and making copy and long after sent a weekly letter to the paper from Washington.[74] Timothy stopped with a very nice Negro family, and had as a friend and companion in his labors, Rev. Luke, a quaint character

Old Customs House, Wilmington, DE. Courtesy of the Delaware Historical Society.

who knew a lot of things worth while. The Norwood family had a fine peach farm near Lewes and Timothy used to spend Sundays with the family and enjoyed it immensely. They had a fine son, S. H. Norwood, who became a minister of the Lord and is still living, I believe, in the Baltimore district.

Much Race Prejudice in State of Delaware

There is a great deal of race prejudice in the State of Delaware. In the rural districts, at the time Timothy was in the State, they were not an educated people, and it is possible that they are not now. In the Presidential election of 1872 Timothy had a chance to see how race prejudice works. The voters approached the election boxes by two lines, the whites on one and the colored on the other. Timothy protested to one of the election officers against some of his high-handed business and came near getting into an election brawl. There were several personal encounters but no general rioting, although there was plenty of combustible sentiment waiting to be set off.[75]

After spending a pleasant summer on the coast, Timothy returned to Wilmington. He had saved enough money to enter college and had sent $100 to the Republican State committee in Florida, as all good office-holders were expected to do in the spoils system. After getting his little affairs in shipshape he resigned the special agency and returned to Washington.

At the age of eighteen Timothy felt himself to be very much a man, but he was woefully uninformed in the rudiments of education, his education having been picked up in printing offices and in much reading of all sorts of literature.

[NJG: November 26, 1927]
After War Times
A Boy's Life in Reconstruction Days—Part 22

Timothy left Wilmington with many regrets. He had many friends there, especially among the younger set, and he had enjoyed life as he found it, with enough money to spend and leisure to enjoy life at its best. But he was bent on entering Howard University, as he was hungry for an education. He little knew that the cards were stacked against him in this hunger, as in many other desires he had for higher and better things, by "the divinity that shapes our ends, rough hew them as we may."[76] Some people just can't have what they desire and earnestly aspire to secure. Like grand old Moses, they are allowed to view but not to enter the Promised Land.

It was easy to enter Howard University in those days, way back in 1877.[77] The school was young, and those who entered it had plenty of zeal for learning but little preparation. General Oliver O. Howard was just giving up the presidency of the school which he had founded and endowed with a princely gift of land, including his private residence, extending from Seventh to Second street and from Florida avenue to the Scheutzen Fest grounds bordering on the Soldiers' Home. It was indeed a princely endowment which the grand old Union soldier made for the higher education of the Afro-American people. John Mercer Langston, a graduate of Oberlin College, a ripe scholar, a brilliant orator and a finished lawyer, who stood next to Frederick Douglass as the potential leader of the Afro-American people, was acting president in the place of General Howard.

Mr. Langston was a very able man. It was the thought and desire of the leaders of the race at that time that he should be selected to succeed General Howard, but those in authority did not think that the time had arrived

Main Building, Howard University, Washington, DC. Prints and Photographs Division, Library of Congress, LC-USZ62-40466.

when a Negro could be made president of such an institution. It was only last year that they changed their mind, after some fifty years of agitation and clamor that they do so.

Race prejudice is a stubborn brute. It dies hard, when it does not live and slime everything it touches and poisons unto death.

Timothy was very illiterate. He was not master even of the primary rudiments, but he had read a great deal and learned much in printing offices and by contact with intelligent people. He was bright and alert enough.[78] He was placed partly in the preparatory department under Professor James Monroe Gregory, with Latin and algebra for study, and in the Normal department under Professor Thomas Robinson, with Miss Martha B. Briggs and Mrs. Keith Bozeman Smith as instructors in grammar, common arithmetic and history. They tried also to impose music and drawing upon him, but he had no liking for them. As to the other studies, he could make but small headway because of lack of training in the rudiments, but he read a great deal of history and biography and some verse, and made a brave showing in the class debating society.[79]

There were some very notable race people at Howard University when Timothy entered it. Besides Acting President Langston there were Professors James Monroe Gregory, C. W. Mitchell, Miss Martha. B. Briggs and Mrs. Keith Bozeman Smith. Mrs. Briggs was one of the most accomplished women of the race I ever knew, a born educator, devoted to the best interests of her pupils, all of whom adored her.[80] Mrs. Smith took a liking for young Timothy and introduced him to her home and to her sisters, and through them Timothy broke into high society, at the head of which towered Frederick Douglass, who loved young people, many of whom gathered about him at his beautiful Cedar Hill home in Anacostia on a certain day in the week, when Mr. Douglass, one of the strongest men of his times, appeared to become as a little child and led the young folks in all of the diversions he prepared in advance for them. When shall we see his like again![81]

Among students at the time who afterwards became useful and famous in education, in the professions and in the ministry, were Former Congressman George H. White, Wiley Lane, George W. Cook, Matthew N. Lewis, Scott Wood, Charles N. and Henry Otey, Dr. F. J. Grimke, James W. Camp, T. J. Shadd, J. H. Merriweather, John W. Eaton, Joseph W. Morris, L. O. Posey, John Nalot [?] and the Misses Nettie Langston (now Mrs. James C. Napier of Nashville), Belle Nelson, Bettie Cox and her friend Mrs. Daniel H. Williams, whose maiden name I do not remember, now of Chicago, and others.

[NJG: December 3, 1927]
After War Times
A Boy's Life in Reconstruction Days
Part 23

How did Timothy finish the college year with no money, after the failure of the Germania Bank? It came about in the following way. Old Man Page, who had the dining room privileges at Howard University, had been a poorhouse keeper in Vermont. He had a red head and a red face and the students he underfed often made him feel red. He knew how to feed students so that they should have a distaste for his feed and be hungry all the time. He would have some bread, cheap meats and diluted coffee for breakfast, molasses and baker's bread and water for lunch, and meat pie for dinner. The menu was regular and did not vary. Those of the students who paid their way without assistance from the college, some twenty-five in number, rebelled against the feed and protested loud and long, but Old Man Page refused to budge and was sustained by the college authorities. The aggrieved students decided to strike. They went across Seventh Street to Mrs. Mason's boarding house and got decent eating with some variety for $12 a month, which was big money in those days.[82]

Mrs. Mason Was a Kindly Soul

Mrs. Mason was a kindly soul who knew her business, and while she did not make much money she made enough to keep her and her family a-going and to apply her husband's earnings on payments on the house they were buying. She did not have much help, and Timothy used to volunteer to draw water for her from the well and to chop wood for her. It was great help, and Timothy had a lot of pleasure in the service. It bound the landlady to him for life, and drew her husband, who was a grand old man, to him in a fatherly way. Of course the "striking students" had to vacate Clark Hall. Timothy roomed and boarded with the Masons. Mr. Mason was a tall stately old man with a patriarchal beard, and was engineer at the Freedman's Bank building, on Pennsylvania avenue opposite the Treasury Building.

When Timothy lost all his money, by the shut down of the bank, Mr. and Mrs. Mason insisted that he go ahead and finish his college year and they would take their money when they could get it and if Timothy could not pay them it would be alright. The old man also gave Timothy what spending money he needed, which was not much, of course. In that way Timothy finished the college year. After some delay and much hustling, Congressman Purman secured for him a place as temporary messenger in the Revenue Marine division of the Treasury, of which Mr. Sumner I. Kimball was chief. The chief took an interest in Timothy, whose attention to his duties as messenger and diligence in reading engaged his notice. He stopped at Timothy's desk one day and scanned the Treasury library book he was perusing, which happened to be "Essays, by Francis Bacon." "You understand that book?" he asked and passed on.[83]

There was another messenger in the Revenue Marine bureau. He was Mr. Warren G. Fearing, who afterwards won a clerkship and was long a successful and helpful citizen of Washington.

Dream To Enter College Now Far Fetched

After paying Mr. and Mrs. Mason out of his earnings of sixty dollars per month as messenger, Timothy saw that he could not enter college the coming term, so he decided to get another job and to read law in the night course.[84] He got a position as compositor of the People's Advocate, owned and edited by Prof. John W. Cromwell, a high priced clerk, who eventually became principal of one of the District schools and the author of some valuable historical writings. He died last year at a ripe old age, after rearing and educating an interesting family. But he could not make the People's Advocate go. Washington was then regarded as the graveyard of Negro newspapers, and it has only been of recent years that better conditions have obtained. And of course Timothy wrote pieces for the People's Advocate, which had among other contributors Mr. Frederick Douglass, Robert Peel Brooks, a brilliant brother of Dr. William H. Brooks, the grand and noble pastor of the Nineteenth Street Baptist Church, in Washington, who has long been the idol of his people and a positive force for good in the life of the District of Columbia, Richard Theodore Greener, Louis H. Douglass, Charles E. Otey and others.[85]

In the mid-winter days Timothy was married, his wages of $40 a month were cut by ten dollars, and he had to cease his law studies and return to Florida and undertake the distasteful work of school teaching.[86] It was four dark and troublous years after that he went to New York and began his career as a journalist, which he is still pursuing under the pen name of T. Thomas Fortune.[87]

And this is the end of the Man Child. The story of the He Man remains to be told some other time and place.

Charlotte ("Carrie") Smiley Fortune. Courtesy of the John Jermain Memorial Library, Sag Harbor, New York, and Elizabeth Bowser.

Afterword

TAMEKA BRADLEY HOBBS

The span of T. Thomas Fortune's life is remarkable. At the height of his career, roughly between 1881 and 1904, he was one of the most respected public intellectuals of his day, considered by many as the "dean" of African American newspaper editors. Unfortunately, with the passage of time, Fortune has too often become a tangent to the better-known careers of Booker T. Washington and Ida B. Wells-Barnett. Despite his historical marginalization, the fact remains that Fortune ran in intellectual and political circles with some of the great race men and women of the late nineteenth and early twentieth centuries, including James Weldon Johnson, W. E. B. DuBois, Josiah T. Walls, John Willis Menard, Alexander Crummell, John Mercer Langston, and Marcus Mosiah Garvey. In the decades after his death in 1928, Fortune's legacy as a journalist and activist has often been overshadowed, partially submerged in the rubble created by the intellectual war between Washington and DuBois, despite being a contemporary and friend of both men. In his full measure, T. Thomas Fortune belongs to the class of great African American thinkers of the nineteenth century and was responsible for advancing ideas about racism and economic justice far ahead of their time, many not taking root until the twentieth century.

The effort to recover Fortune's legacy continues with the publication of his collection of essays, "After War Times." While less celebrated than Fortune's earlier writings, taken as a whole, these essays reveal much about his early life and circumstances, especially his recounting of the promise and decline of the Reconstruction era. More dramatically, it includes a vivid firsthand account of his family's battles with white terrorists in Marianna, Florida, as the county descended into deadly contests for political control.

Clockwise from upper left: T. Thomas Fortune, Booker T. Washington, Ida B. Wells, John Mitchell, and (center) Frederick Douglass. (Henry D. Northrop, Joseph Gay, Garlane Penn, *The College of Life, or Practical Self-Educator: A Manual of Self-Improvement for the Colored Race*. Horace C. Fry Publisher, 1896.)

His own father, Emanuel Fortune Sr., a local Republican activist, became the target of murderous threats. Despite these and other tribulations, Fortune's writing describes his family's striving to make the most of their new condition. Emanuel Fortune, who as an enslaved man worked as a tanner and shoemaker, fought hard as a freed man to support this family while also using his talents as a leader in Marianna's civic community. His wife, Sarah, determined to care for her children, enrolled them in a school operated by the Freedmen's Bureau.[1]

Young Tim, as he was called, drank deeply from these founts of character and as a young man engaged his own work ethic and intellect, coupled with his father's reputation and connections, to make a way for himself. Hardworking, capable, and a student of mankind and human nature, Fortune received a valuable education in politics and journalism while in Tallahassee, in addition to making favorable impressions on the many Republicans, black and white, in the state legislature. As it turned out, these connections from the state capitol in Tallahassee helped link him to federal resources in the nation's capital.

It is also during these years that Fortune began to learn the skills of a printer, working for a number of newspapers in Marianna, Tallahassee, and Jacksonville. He later credited the technical and rhetorical skills that he learned while employed in newspaper offices in Florida and Washington, DC,—beyond the scant two years he spent at Howard University—as the greatest contribution to his educational advancement. The political reversals after the election of 1876 translated into less direct federal support for Howard University and fewer government employment opportunities for their students. This left Fortune unable to pay for his education. After his marriage to Carrie Smiley of Jacksonville in 1877, Fortune took a brief foray into teaching, an occupation to which he never aspired and described as "distasteful." Moreover the relative freedom and urbanity he experienced while in the nation's capital made it impossible for him to abide the regressive racial policies of his home state. He soon sought refuge in New York City.

It is ironic that the chronology in Fortune's "After War Times" essays concludes just before he launched into the most productive and successful years of his public career as a journalist and "race man." It is during this time that he established himself as a national figure in the African American community. Once in New York City, Fortune found employment at the *Weekly Witness*, a white-owned paper. Later he took on the editorship of the African American weekly tabloid *Rumor*, which would become the *Globe*. By 1884, the *Globe* ceased printing and a few weeks later Fortune launched the New York *Freeman*, of which he served as sole proprietor and editor. He also began to work as a freelance journalist for the *New York Tribune*, once published by Horace Greeley, as well as the *New York Sun*, published by Charles Dana. Later in 1887, the *Freeman* transformed into the New York *Age*.

Fortune earned a reputation for his sharp wit, pointed and unflinching criticism of racism and inequality, and a consistent commitment to the advancement of African Americans. The pages of the *Age* became Fortune's soapbox, from which he hurled invective at those who sought to hamper the advancement of the black race, including politicians of all stripes, lynch mobs, and corrupt African American leaders. Fortune's work brought him into contact with other race leaders, resulting in both the exchange of ideas and ideological clashes.

In 1884 Fortune published his *magnum opus* on race relations, *Black and White: Land, Labor, and Politics in the South*. In it, he deftly combined sociological, macroeconomic, political, and historical commentary on the subject of black southern life. In addition to its breadth of subject matter and astute observations, Fortune's writing blended high ideas and plain language, peppered with helpings of biblical references, folk sayings, polished rhetoric, and sarcasm. A central concern in the work is the issue of race in the South, especially the uphill battle that African Americans faced as they attempted to regain their civil rights without the support of the federal government, a theme he returned to in "After War Times." Fortune dedicated equal energy to his unflinching criticism of the nation's failure to protect the voting and civil rights of African Americans from the lawless and violent encroachments of white southerners. He demanded full citizenship rights for African Americans, a line of thought Susan Carle links to his tutelage under John Mercer Langston, who served at the helm of Howard University during Fortune's brief tenure there. Both men defended the right of a black man to cast a ballot as well as his right to attend a public theater or to be served in a restaurant.[2]

Beyond these topics, however, Fortune expounded at considerable length on the dangers posed by concentration of wealth in the hands of the few. His criticism focused on the tyrants of industry—coal, railroad, and banking—who he claimed, with the complicity of politicians, ran roughshod over the nation's working class, irrespective of color. Fortune also was a firm believer in equal economic opportunity; his experiences during slavery and Reconstruction provided clear examples of the vulnerability faced by those without land or wealth.

Deeply influenced by the socialist thought of Edward Kellogg, Karl Marx, and others, Fortune championed the dignity of labor and the (quite

Jeffersonian) notion that future success of the nation rested in Americans' ability to own and retain enough land to sustain themselves and their families. As a result, the theme of economic justice formed a significant tenet within Fortune's advocacy, as he understood that the law alone could not permanently advance the place of African Americans in American society. As Susan Carle points out, Fortune melded both progressive and conservative ideologies in a way that advocated "retaining the institutions of democracy but working through them for government interventions that would redistribute economic resources and lessen the consequences of preexisting social and economic inequality."[3]

Within this same vein of equal opportunity, Fortune voiced support for the Knights of Labor, one of the nation's leading labor unions, which had recently begun accepting African Americans as members, albeit in segregated units. It is no surprise that he was attracted to the group, as it embodied two ideologies that were close to Fortune's heart—interracial cooperation and economic fairness. Fortune also vocally supported the education bill sponsored by Senator Henry W. Blair, which sought to distribute federal aid to fund education in individual states based on rates of illiteracy. Fortune spoke before the Senate Committee reviewing the bill, taking the view that "the education of the people is a legitimate function of Government and is not in any sense a feature of centralization, but is eminently a feature of self preservation."[4] While Fortune continued to speak and write in favor of the bill, true to his principled stand on equal rights, he maintained his objection to the continuation of segregated schools.

Of the numerous issues T. Thomas Fortune championed in his career, he stood steadfast on the principle of equal rights for African Americans. Having witnessed the great strides accomplished during the post-bellum period, he grieved the erosion of the protections enacted in the progressive Reconstruction amendments, especially when the US Supreme Court handed down its devastating decisions in *Pace v. Alabama*, the *Civil Rights Cases*, and *Plessy v. Ferguson*.[5] To combat the regression, Fortune envisioned an organization that could initiate and fund court cases to challenge these misinterpretations and reestablish the protections intended by the Fourteenth and Fifteenth amendments to the US Constitution. To work toward these aims, Fortune organized the National Afro-American League (NAAL) in 1887, with an ambitious and aggressive agenda, including an effort to secure the voting rights of black men, equal access for blacks in transportation and public accommodations, equal funding for schools, and criminal justice for

African Americans in order to combat lynching and convict leasing. In the end, the NAAL proved to be a short-lived effort, only surviving for three years. Fortune and Rev. Alexander Walter revived the effort in 1898 as the National Afro-American Council (NAAC). This slightly less militant organization proved more stable, perhaps due to the support and influence of Booker T. Washington.

Despite the relative cohesion of this new group, leaders like DuBois, Wells, and journalist William Monroe Trotter, dissatisfied with the conservative nature of the NAAC, bolted and organized under the umbrella of the Niagara Movement. With the collapse of the Niagara Movement, the vision for a national civil rights organization was inherited by the National Association for the Advancement of Colored People (NAACP) in 1909, which would become the nation's premier civil rights organization. While unable to hold together the fabric of the movement he envisioned, there is no doubt that Fortune served as the intellectual godfather of the subsequent efforts to achieve equal protection under the law for African Americans.

Tied to the fight for civil and social rights, Fortune remained a fierce advocate for the dignity and respect of African Americans. This is evidenced by his debate with other black intellectuals of the time over the semantics of race; rejecting the use of the terms "negro" and "colored," Fortune instead advocated the use of "Afro-American," which, in his view, most accurately represented the history and condition of people of African descent in America. Interestingly, while continually demonstrating pride of race in his writings and speeches, one significant component of Fortune's writing in *Black and White* and his later writings were predictions of a postracial future for the South and by implication the entire country. In his view, amalgamation was a natural and necessary consequence of his ultimate vision of civic and social equality, postulating that for all Americans "[t]he color of their skin must cease to be an index to their political creed. They must think less of the party and more of themselves give less heed to a name and more heed to principles."[6] This line of thinking was perhaps inspired by his own multiethnic heritage—African, Native American, Jewish, and Irish—and also explains his defense of interracial marriages.

The pages of the *Age* frequently included reports of racial violence and lynching. His strong association with the antilynching movement would be cemented further when he offered a home to Ida B. Wells in 1892. Wells, publisher of the Memphis *Free Speech and Headlight*, found herself a fugitive from her native South after writing editorials indicting the lawlessness of the lynch mob but also, by extension, hinting at the complicity of southern white women in the violence, insinuating that their attraction to black men might be at the root of the supposed menace of the black rapist. Whites in Memphis destroyed Wells's press and threatened her life if she returned to the city. It would be Fortune who offered her a job writing for the New York *Age* and assisted her in settling in her temporarily adopted home.[7]

One of the more controversial issues surrounding Fortune's career is his relationship with Booker T. Washington. The two men shared very similar backgrounds, both being born into slavery and witnessing firsthand the transition from slavery to freedom. Both, through hard work, educated and supported themselves. Because of their work experience, both tended to promote the value of technical education over liberal arts. Fortune supported Washington and his work at Tuskegee, even before Washington's star rose in the aftermath of his 1895 speech at the Cotton States and International Exposition in Atlanta, making him the foremost authority on African Americans. Sounding very much like Washington, Fortune warned against blacks pursuing what he considered dead-end careers: "To educate him for a lawyer when there are no clients for medicine when the patients although numerous are too poor to give him a living income to fill his head with Latin and Greek as a teacher when the people he is to teach are to be instructed in the abcs such education is a waste of time and a senseless expenditure of money."[8]

In some regards the relationship seemed to be an odd pairing. Apart from their backgrounds and their ideas about education, the two men exhibited two very different public temperaments. While Washington made his name and staked his reputation on appeals to southern blacks for accommodation to the racial status quo, Fortune seemed irrepressible in his desire for legal equality for African Americans. Where Washington was diplomatic and self-effacing, Fortune was abrasive and direct. As with most relationships of convenience, the two men were bound to each other by their reciprocal expectations. Washington counted on Fortune to use the pages of the *Age* to offer support for his agenda and programs, especially in light of growing criticism of his go-slow approach to civil rights. Washington also took advantage of Fortune's skills as a writer, enlisting him as a ghostwriter on at least two works—*A New Negro for a New Century: An Accurate Up-To-Date Record of the Upward Struggles of the Negro Race* (published in 1900) and *The Negro in Business* (published in 1907).[9] On the other hand, Fortune became dependent on Washington's financial largesse to support his foundering paper. Furthermore, he hoped that, through Washington's influence and connections with politicians in Washington, DC, he could obtain appointment to a federal post, providing him with a stable income.[10] This arrangement was not a relationship between equals, and in 1907 Washington would exploit Fortune's economic vulnerability to oust him and take over complete control of the *Age*.

The signs of T. Thomas Fortune's decline began to manifest in or around 1907. Around that time he began to exhibit erratic behavior that was coupled by increasing dependence on alcohol. Termed then as a "nervous breakdown," Fortune exhibited signs that would be recognized today as bipolar disorder, or manic depression. This condition complicated his already precarious financial situation. It was also during these years that Fortune separated from his wife and children, perhaps a sign of his increasing instability. As Fortune fell off balance, Booker T. Washington proceeded to secretly purchase Fortune's share of the *Age*. Unfortunately the man known as the "dean of African American editors" took years to recover from these setbacks.

Over the next several years, Fortune worked as a freelance journalist, publishing with a number of newspapers on the east coast. After writing for the *Norfolk Journal and Guide*, Fortune assumed the position of editor of the paper in 1922. The following year he began to edit the *Negro World*, the news organ for Marcus M. Garvey's Universal Negro Improvement Association (UNIA), a post he would hold until his death in 1928. Fortune's attraction to Garvey was natural; the success of the UNIA confirmed for him the validity of his own ideas about racial pride and self-determination.[11] It was certainly a belated but powerful vindication of Fortune's lifelong efforts for the advancement of African Americans.

Examined *in toto*, T. Thomas Fortune's accomplishments as a journalist and activist cement his position as one of the premier race leaders of the late nineteenth and early twentieth centuries. Beyond that, Fortune set forth a visionary agenda for racial and societal advancement around the issue of civil rights, a mantle that would ultimately be assumed and carried out by the NAACP and other activist organizations. His bold ideas and the precedent of his courage stand as positive examples of what a committed public intellectual could and should be. Fortune, in the end, proved to be, simultaneously, a man ahead of his time and a man for the ages.

Appendix

Bartow Black

By T. Thomas Fortune
Editor *New York Freeman*

'Twas when the Proclamation came,—
Far in the sixties back,—
He left his lord, and changed his name
To "Mister Bartow Black."

He learned to think himself a man,
And privileged, you know,
To adopt a new and different plan,—
To lay aside the hoe.

He took the lead in politics,
And handled all the "notes,"—
For he was up to all the tricks
That gather in the votes;

For when the war came to a close
And negroes "took a stand,"
Young Bartow with the current rose,
The foremost in command.

His voice upon the "stump" was heard;
He "Yankeedom" did prate;
The "carpet-bagger" he revered;
The Southerner did hate.

He now was greater than the lord
Who used to call him slave,
For he was on the "County Board,"
With every right to rave.

But this amazing run of luck
Was far too good to stand;
And soon the chivalrous "Ku-Klux"
Rose in the Southern land.

Then Bartow got a little note,—
'Twas very queerly signed,—
It simply told him not to vote,
Or be to death resigned.

Young Bartow thought this little game
Was very fine and nice
To bring his courage rare to shame
And knowledge of justice.

"What right have they to think I fear?"
He to himself did say.
"Dare they presume that I do care
How loudly they do bray?

"This is my home, and here I die,
Contending for my right!
Then let them come! My colors fly!
I'm ready now to fight!

"Let those who think that Bartow Black,—
An office-holder, too!—
Will to the cowards show his back,
Their vain presumption rue!"

Bartow pursued his office game,
And made the money, too,
But home at nights he wisely came
And played the husband true.

When they had got their subject tame,
And well-matured their plan,

They at the hour of midnight came,
And armed was every man!

They numbered fifty Southern sons,
And masked was every face;
And Winfield rifles were their guns,—
You could that plainly trace.

One Southern brave did have a key,
An entrance quick to make;
They entered all; but meek, you see,
Their victim not to wake!

They reached his room! He was in
bed,—
His wife was by his side!
They struck a match above his head,—
His eyes he opened wide!

Poor Bartow could not reach his gun,
Though quick his arm did stretch,
For twenty bullets through him spun,
That stiffly laid the wretch.

And then they rolled his carcass o'er,
And filled both sides with lead;
And then they turned it on the floor,
And shot away his head!

Ere Black his bloody end did meet
His wife had swooned away;
The Southern braves did now retreat,—
There was no need to stay!

—AME Church Review 3, October, 1886, pp. 158–59

Fortune appended the following note to the poem: "The facts upon which this poem is based are substantially correct. Black was well known to me, by his proper name, Calvin Rogers. He was far above the average of his race in intelligence and courage. He was killed, as here described, in Jackson County, Florida (where I was born), in the early part of 1870, a reference to which can be found in volume 13, page 192, of the "Ku-Klux Conspiracy," reported to Congress in 1872 by the Joint Select Committee."

Notes

Introduction

1. Emma Lou Thornbrough, *T. Thomas Fortune: Militant Journalist* (Chicago: University of Chicago Press, 1972); Shawn Leigh Alexander, ed., *T. Thomas Fortune, the Afro-American Agitator* (Gainesville: University Press of Florida, 2008), xii; *New York Times*, June 4, 1900. As to Fortune's poetry and prose published in book form, see Timothy Thomas Fortune, *Black and White: Land, Labor, and Politics in the South* (New York: Fords, Howard, & Hubert, 1884); idem, *Dreams of Life* (New York: Fortune & Peterson, 1905).

2. Jerrell H. Shofner, *Jackson County, Florida—A History* (Marianna, FL: Jackson County Heritage Association, 1985), 1–218; Joseph C. G. Kennedy, comp., *Population of the United States in 1860; Compiled from the Original Returns of the Eighth Census* (Washington, DC: Government Printing Office, 1864), 54; Francis A. Walker, comp., *Ninth Census—Volume 1: The Statistics of the Population of the United States* (Washington, DC: Government Printing Office, 1872), 98. The principal works on the Middle Florida plantation region and the institution of slavery within it include Julia Floyd Smith, *Slavery and Plantation Growth in Antebellum Florida, 1821–1860* (Gainesville: University Press of Florida, 1973); Edward E. Baptist, *Creating an Old South: Middle Florida's Plantation Frontier before the Civil War* (Chapel Hill: University of North Carolina Press, 2002); Larry Eugene Rivers, *Slavery in Florida: Territorial Days to Emancipation* (Gainesville: University Press of Florida, 2000); idem, *Rebels and Runaways: Slave Resistance in Florida* (Urbana: University of Illinois Press, 2012).

3. Thornbrough, *T. Thomas Fortune*, 34; Cyrus Field Adams, "Timothy Thomas Fortune: Journalist, Author, Lecturer, Agitator," *Colored American Magazine* 4 (January and February 1902), 225; Shofner, *Jackson County*, 143; Gene M. Burnett, *Florida's Past: People and Events that Shaped the State, Volume 1* (Sarasota, FL: Pineapple Press, 1986), 51.

4. Adams, "Timothy Thomas Fortune," 225.

5. *New York Age*, March 8, 1890; Adams, "Timothy Thomas Fortune," 225.

6. Shofner, *Jackson County*, 219–52; *Norfolk* (VA) *Journal and Guide*, July 23, 1927. On the Battle of Marianna, see Dale Cox, *The Battle of Marianna, Florida: Expanded Edition* (Fort Smith, AR: priv. pub., 2011). On Union operations in the Florida Panhandle region during 1864 and 1865, including the raid on Marianna, see David J. Coles, "Far from the Fields of Glory: Military Operations in Florida during the Civil War" (PhD dissertation, Florida State University, 1996).

7. Armstrong Purdee, "Eye-Witness Tells of Burning of Church," *Kalendar* (Men's Club, St. Luke's Episcopal Church, Marianna, Florida) 1 (June 1, 1931), available online at http://www.rootsweb.ancestry.com/~flgatsaa/kalendar.html; Susie King Taylor, *Reminiscences of My Life in Camp with the 33d United States Colored Troops, Late 1st S.C. Volunteers* (Boston: priv. pub., 1902); idem, *Reminiscences of My Life: A Black Woman's Civil War Memoirs*, ed. by Patricia W. Romero and Willie Lee Rose (New York: Markus Wiener Publishing, 1988).

8. Taylor, *Reminiscences of My Life* (1988), 135.

9. Canter Brown Jr., *Florida's Black Public Officials, 1867–1924* (Tuscaloosa: University of Alabama Press, 1998), x; personal interview, Canter Brown Jr., by Dawn Herd-Clark, July 6, 2011 (notes in collection of Dawn Herd-Clark). See also Joe M. Richardson, *The Negro in the Reconstruction of Florida, 1865–1877* (Tallahassee: Florida State University Press, 1965; reprint ed., Tampa: Trend House, 1973); Canter Brown Jr., *Ossian Bingley Hart: Florida's Loyalist Reconstruction Governor* (Baton Rouge: Louisiana State University Press, 1997); Larry Eugene Rivers and Canter Brown Jr., *Laborers in the Vineyard of the Lord: The Beginnings of the AME Church in Florida, 1865–1895* (Gainesville: University Press of Florida, 2001); Canter Brown Jr., and Larry Eugene Rivers, *For a Great and Grand Purpose: The Beginnings of the AMEZ Church in Florida, 1864–1905* (Gainesville: University Press of Florida, 2004). An interesting and important narrative from the perspective of an Africa-born Floridian and relating to the state's antebellum experience in the St. Augustine vicinity recently has become available. See Sitiki, *The Odyssey of an African Slave*, ed. by Patricia C. Griffin (Gainesville: University Press of Florida, 2009).

10. Garland I. Penn, *The Afro-American Press, and Its Editors* (Springfield, MA: Willey & Co., 1891), 103–4; Henry Lewis Suggs, ed., *The Black Press in the South, 1865–1979* (Westport, CT: Greenwood Press, 1983), 91; *Philadelphia North American and United States Gazette*, August 24, 1872; Larry Eugene Rivers and Canter Brown Jr., "John Willis Menard and *Lays in Summer Lands*" in John Willis Menard, *Lays in Summer Lands*, ed. by Larry Eugene Rivers, Richard Mathews, and Canter Brown Jr. (Tampa: University of Tampa Press, 2002), 95–96; John T. Shuften, *A Colored Man's Exposition of the Acts and Doings of the Radical Party of the South, From 1865 to 1876, And Its Probable Overthrow By President Hayes' Southern Policy* (Jacksonville, FL: Gibson & Dennis, 1877).

11. Maxine D. Jones and Kevin M. McCarthy, *African Americans in Florida*

(Sarasota, FL: Pineapple Press, 1993), 42–43; Adams, "Timothy Thomas Fortune," 226; *Washington* (DC) *National Republican*, June 10, 1876. On Josiah Walls, see Peter B. Klingman, *Josiah Walls: Florida's Black Congressman of Reconstruction* (Gainesville: University of Florida Press, 1976).

12. Brown, *Florida's Black Public Officials*, 134–35. Historians have speculated on the degree to which *Carpetbag Rule in Florida* was shaped or even written by white politicians who used Wallace's work to settle old scores; see James C. Clark, "John Wallace and the Writing of Reconstruction History," *Florida Historical Quarterly* 67 (April 1989), 409–27; Larry Eugene Rivers and Canter Brown Jr., "Attorney John Wallace: Pioneering the Profession of Law within Florida's African American Community," *Journal of the Georgia Association of Historians* 30 (2011), 1–53; John Wallace, *Carpetbag Rule in Florida: The Inside Workings of the Reconstruction of Civil Government in Florida After the Close of the Civil War* (Jacksonville, FL: Da Costa Printing and Publishing Company, 1888; reprint ed., Kennesaw, GA: Continental Book Co., 1959), 4, 108. The Jackson County War and the local activities of William J. Purman and Charles M. Hamilton have received considerable attention and sparked continuing controversies. Among other sources, see Shofner, *Jackson County*, 253–320; Daniel R. Weinfeld, *The Jackson County War: Reconstruction and Resistance in Post–Civil War Florida* (Tuscaloosa: University of Alabama Press, 2012); idem, "'More Courage than Discretion': Charles M. Hamilton in Reconstruction-Era Florida," *Florida Historical Quarterly* 84 (Spring 2006), 479–516.

13. Rivers and Brown, "John Willis Menard," 103–15. On John Willis Menard, see also Edith Menard, "John Willis Menard, First Negro Elected to the U.S. Congress, First Negro to Speak in the U.S. Congress," *Negro History Bulletin* 18 (December 1964), 53–54; Bess Beatty, "John Willis Menard: A Progressive Black in Post–Civil War Florida," *Florida Historical Quarterly* 59 (October 1980), 123–43.

14. J. Willis Menard, *Lays in Summer Lands* (Washington, DC: Enterprise Publishing Co., 1879); Fortune, *Dreams of Life*; Jerrell H. Shofner, "Florida," in *The Black Press in the South, 1865–1979*, ed. by Henry Lewis Suggs (Westport, CT: Greenwood Press, 1983), 92–93; Rivers and Brown, "John Willis Menard," 110–15.

15. Shofner, "Florida," 92–93; Rivers and Brown, "John Willis Menard," 113–16; *New York Age*, November 16, 1889.

16. James Weldon Johnson, *Along This Way: The Autobiography of James Weldon Johnson* (New York: Viking Penguin, 1933; reprint ed., New York: Penguin Group, 1990), 48–49, 58.

17. See Dorothy Dodd, "'Bishop' Pearce and the Reconstruction of Leon County," *Apalachee* (1946), 5–12; Rivers and Brown, *Laborers in the Vineyard of the Lord*; Brown, *Florida's Black Public Officials*, 115.

18. Brown, *Florida's Black Public Officials*, 76, 109–110; ibid., "Where are now

the hopes I cherished? The Life and Times of Robert Meacham," *Florida Historical Quarterly* 69 (July 1990), 1–36. See also, Rivers and Brown, *Laborers in the Vineyard of the Lord.*

19. Darius J. Young, "Henry S. Harmon: Pioneer African American Attorney in Reconstruction-Era Florida," *Florida Historical Quarterly* 85 (Fall 2006), 177–96; Larry E. Rivers, "'He Treats His Fellow Man Properly': Building Community in Multi-Cultural Florida," in *Amid Political, Cultural, and Civic Diversity: Building a Sense of Statewide Community in Florida*, ed. by Lance deHaven-Smith and David Colburn (Dubuque, IA: Kendall/Hunt, 1998).

20. *New York Freeman*, April 11, 1885; Johnson, *Along This Way* 58, 137; Ledell W. Neyland and John W. Riley, *The History of Florida Agricultural and Mechanical University* (Gainesville: University of Florida Press, 1963), 14, 40.

21. William Watson Davis, *The Civil War and Reconstruction in Florida* (New York: Columbia University Press, 1913; reprint ed., Gainesville: University of Florida Press, 1964); William Edward Burghardt DuBois, *Black Reconstruction in America, 1860–1880* (New York: Atheneum, 1935); Richardson, *Negro in the Reconstruction of Florida*; Jerrell H. Shofner, *Nor Is It over Yet: Florida in the Era of Reconstruction, 1863–1877* (Gainesville: University of Florida Press, 1974); Edward C. Williamson, *Florida Politics during the Gilded Age, 1877–1893* (Gainesville: University Presses of Florida, 1976).

22. Joe M. Richardson, "The Freedmen's Bureau and Negro Education in Florida," *Journal of Negro Education* 31 (Autumn 1962), 460–67. On the Freedmen's Bureau generally, see, for example, W. E. Burghardt DuBois, "The Freedmen's Bureau," *Atlantic Monthly* 87 (March 1901), 354–65; George R. Bentley, *A History of the Freedmen's Bureau* (Philadelphia: University of Pennsylvania, 1955); Paul A. Cimbala, *The Freedmen's Bureau: Reconstructing the American South after the Civil War* (Malabar, FL: Krieger Publishing Company, 2005); Mary Farmer-Kaiser, *Freedwomen and the Freedmen's Bureau: Race, Gender, and Public Policy in the Age of Emancipation* (New York: Fordham University Press, 2010).

23. Brown, *Florida's Black Public Officials*, 88–89.

24. US Congress, *Index to the Reports of the Committees of the Senate of the United States for the Second Session Forty Second Congress, 1871–1872*, 42nd Cong., 2nd sess., 1872, Committee Print, 94.

25. *Topeka* (KS) *Plaindealer*, June 15, 1928.

Editor's Note

1. T. Thomas Fortune to Booker T. Washington, Oct. 13, 1899, in Louis R. Harlan and Raymond W. Smock, eds., *Booker T. Washington Papers*, vol. 5 (Urbana: University of Illinois Press, 1976), 233.

2. Catherine Clinton argues that the "Mammy" figure rarely existed before emancipation, but rather was a post–Civil War "figment of the combined romantic imaginations of the contemporary southern ideologue and the modern southern historian." Harris's creation of the Aunt Minervy Ann character, more than thirty years after emancipation, corroborates Clinton's assertion. Catherine Clinton, *The Plantation Mistress* (New York: Pantheon Books, 1982), 2012.

3. Fortune, who claimed European, African, and Seminole forebears, probably took offense at Harris's derogatory comments about "mulatters" and harsh disparagement of an "Injun mulatter." Harris depicts mulattos as distinct from African Americans. Unlike southern blacks, whom Harris portrays as essentially content with their subservient place in the racial hierarchy, mulattos are subversive and dangerous: they seek power, ally themselves with the invading carpetbaggers, and inveigle malleable blacks to collude in their corrupt schemes. Joel Chandler Harris, *The Chronicles of Aunt Minervy Ann* (New York: Charles Scribner and Sons, 1899), 108, 111–14, 185.

4. No ready explanation exists for the nearly three-decade gap between Fortune's announcement of his intention to write "After War Times" and its actual publication. It can be guessed that Fortune's suspicion of the memoir form played a role in the delay. Autobiographies, Fortune had commented, "are hazardous things to write, and few men have done more than make themselves ridiculous for all time by indulging in the weakness." *New York Sun*, Nov. 21, 1897.

5. *Norfolk Journal and Guide*, June 9, 1928.

After War Times

1. The 1860 US Census slave schedule for Jackson County, FL, lists a five-year-old mulatto boy residing in the home of merchant Eli P. Moore. Eighth Census of the United States, 1860, Jackson County, Florida. A major hurricane directly struck Jackson County and the Florida Panhandle on August 31, 1856, just one month before Fortune's birth. US Department of Commerce, National Oceanic and Atmospheric Administration, http://www.aoml.noaa.gov/hrd/hurdat/figs_tables.htm.

2. A tombstone for "Sarah Jane wife of E. Fortune Sr." located in Jacksonville's Old City Cemetery lists a birth date of July 4, 1838, which is consistent with the 1860 US Census Jackson County slave schedule and the 1870 US Census from Duval County, FL. http://www.findagrave.com. An 1866 marriage certificate on file at the Jackson County Florida Courthouse lists "Sarah J. Mires." One account, probably written by Fortune, described Sarah Jane as "a small, wiry woman, of splendid figure and beauty, and with a strength of character not often found in a woman slave." Many considered her "the most beautiful woman in Jackson county,

Florida." Adams, "Timothy Thomas Fortune," 225. Eighth Census of the United States, 1860, Jackson County, Florida; Ninth Census of the United States, 1870, Duval County, Florida.

3. Roger Brooke Taney (1877–1864) was appointed chief justice of the US Supreme Court in 1836 by President Andrew Jackson and held that position until his death. In his 1857 decision in the case of *Dred Scott v. Sandford*, Taney took the opportunity presented by the question of the status of slavery in the territories to observe that the founders of the nation had considered black people "an inferior order . . . and so far unfit that they had no rights which the white man was bound to respect." Taney concluded that blacks could not be considered citizens "within the meaning of the Constitution." *Dred Scott v. Sandford*, 60 US 393 (1857). Fortune considered the 1859 raid by John Brown (1800–1859) on the armory at Harpers Ferry "a heroic effort to break the chains of the bondsman." T. Thomas Fortune, *New York Age*, Jan. 25, 1890, in Alexander, *T. Thomas Fortune, Afro-American Agitator*, 136–37.

4. Frederick Douglass (1818–1895) escaped slavery to become the most recognizable African American leader and abolitionist. Fortune considered Douglass to be the "greatest man of his race." *New York Sun*, Nov. 21, 1897. Abraham Lincoln (1809–1865): sixteenth president of the United States.

5. The first evidence of Emanuel Fortune's political activity and stature as a leader came in March 1867 when his signature appeared at the head of the names of sixty-eight Jackson County African American men who petitioned Florida's Freedman's Bureau Assistant Commissioner Col. John T. Sprague to request the return of William J. Purman to Jackson County after the Bureau transferred Purman to the state's east coast. In late July 1867, the Jackson County Bureau officers selected Fortune as the single black member of the county's three-member voter registration board, making him the first African American appointed to a government position in Jackson County. In the same month, Fortune was also appointed to a committee of six men, comprised of three whites and three blacks, to supervise the funding and construction of a schoolhouse in Marianna. In November, Jackson County voters, mostly black, elected Fortune to be one of four Jackson County delegates to the state constitutional convention to be held in Tallahassee in January 1868. At the convention, Fortune and three other black delegates aligned with William J. Purman's "moderate" Republican faction in opposition to the "radical" or "mule team" faction. In May 1868, Jackson County voters elected Fortune as their representative to serve for three sessions in the Florida state legislature (1868, 1869, 1870). He was appointed sergeant-of-arms to the same body in 1872. Biographies list Emanuel Fortune's birth date as January 3, 1832, but obituaries and his own statement during the Congressional KKK Hearings indicate that he was born the following year. Petition of Jackson County, Florida, Freedmen to Col. John T. Sprague, March 25, 1867; C. M. Hamilton to O. B. Hart, July 27, 1867; W. J.

Purman to C. Thurston Chase, Aug. 3, 1867; Records of the Assistant Commissioner and Subordinate field offices for the State of Florida, Bureau of Refugees, Freedmen, and Abandoned Lands 1865–1872 (microform), Department of Special Collections, Smathers Library, University of Florida, Gainesville (hereinafter cited as Records, Florida, BRF&AL); Brown, *Florida's Black Public Officials*, 8, 10, 88–89; "Testimony Taken by the Joint Select Committee to Inquire Into the Condition of Affairs in the Late Insurrectionary States," House Report No. 22, pt. 13, 42d Cong., 2d sess. (Washington, DC 1872), 94 (hereinafter cited as *House Report No. 22*); A Journal of the Proceedings of the Assembly of the State of Florida, 1868–1873; *New York Sun*, January 28, 1897; *Cleveland Gazette*, February 6, 1897.

6. According to Adams's biography, Thomas Fortune, an Irish adventurer, lived "only about one year in the county, when he was killed in a pistol duel with a planter. He was a highly educated but quick-tempered man, and not fitted to endure the hauteur of the slave master class among whom he drifted by chance." Adams, "Timothy Thomas Fortune," 225. "Thomas M. Fortune" appears in the 1830 Jackson County Florida Census, but this Fortune does not appear to have played a significant role in the Seminole Wars. Jackson County historian J. Randall Stanley wrote that Adam Fortune, who was listed together with Thomas M. Fortune in the 1830 Census, had owned Emanuel Fortune as a slave, but Stanley offered no evidence to support this claim. Fifth Census of the United States, 1830, Jackson County, Florida. J. Randall Stanley, *History of Jackson County* (Marianna, FL: Jackson County Historical Society, 1950), 215.

7. Many popular legends are associated with Osceola, the renowned Seminole leader, including the tale that his wife, the daughter of an escaped slave and a Seminole chief, had been seized by whites on behalf of her mother's former master. Kenneth W. Porter, "The Episode of Osceola's Wife," *Florida Historical Quarterly* 26 (July 1947), 92. This story, appearing in print as early as 1837, continued to be repeated in antislavery publications. *The Quarterly Anti-Slavery Magazine*, vol. II, (July 1837), 419; *American Anti-Slavery Almanac* (1839); Rev. William Goodell, *Slavery and Anti-Slavery* (1852), 270; Joshua R. Giddings, *The Exiles of Florida* (1858), 98–99. As indicated by a reference in the preface to his collection of poems, *Dreams of Life*, Fortune was quite familiar with Giddings's book. Thorough investigation, however, has demonstrated that, while plausible, the veracity of this story about Osceola's wife is very doubtful. Porter, *Osceola's Wife*, 95; Patricia R. Wickman, *Osceola's Legacy* (Tuscaloosa: University of Alabama Press, 2006), 58. In any event, the chronology of the accounts does not correspond to Emanuel Fortune's birth in 1833 and the outbreak of the Second Seminole War in 1835. This family legend is significant in that it reflects the family's interest in linking itself with the illustrious, romanticized Osceola who bravely, though futilely, resisted the attempt of the United States to control and resettle the Seminole people. A biographical profile of T. Thomas Fortune, predating the "After War Times" series

by twenty-five years, states that Emanuel had Seminole ancestors but does not mention a connection to Osceola. Adams, "Timothy Thomas Fortune," 225. And Fortune, too, is inconsistent: in two articles he wrote that discuss the story of Osceola at length and include the legend of the abduction of the chief's wife, Fortune does not invoke a family connection. *New York Sun*, May 12, 1895, June 20, 1897.

8. Rev. John Pope was an early adherent in Florida of the African Methodist Episcopal Church. He was one of the preachers admitted to the church at its annual Florida conference in March 1868 and was appointed pastor of Sim's Harbor in the Marianna District. Rivers and Brown, *Laborers in the Vineyard of the Lord,* 53–54. The 1870 census lists John Pope as a Tennessee-born, seventy-five-year-old black "AME preacher" married to seventy-three-year-old Docia, who is listed as mulatto and born in South Carolina. Ninth Census of the United States, 1870, Jackson County, Florida.

9. 2 Corinthians 5:1.

10. At the time of the Civil War, Eli P. Moore was a partner of Alderman, Moore and Company, selling "dry goods, drugs, paints, books and stationery." Jerrell H. Shofner, *Jackson County,* 127. Fortune's memory was remarkable: in the 1860 US Census, Moore, then thirty-nine, and his wife, Elizabeth, were listed with one son, Thomas, born 1849, and three daughters, Ruth, born 1851; Julia, born 1857; and Sarah, born about 1860. The 1860 slave schedules list Moore as owning four slaves; males ages forty-three and five, and females ages twenty-one and three, all described as "mulatto." The children are presumably T. Thomas Fortune and his sister, Martha. Eighth Census of the United States, 1860, Jackson County, Florida.

11. The white male population of Jackson County, Florida, included about 1,400 men whose ages would have made them subject to service and eventual conscription in the Confederate forces. Many enlisted in the Florida regiments dispatched to General Robert E. Lee's Army of Northern Virginia or the Confederate armies of the Western theater, while others served in the home guard or units that did not leave Florida. Approximately 20 percent of these Jackson County men died in the Civil War, from disease or combat.

12. In September 1864, a column of eight hundred Union soldiers led by the Hungarian-born General Alexander Asboth ventured from their Pensacola base to cross the Florida Panhandle with the goal destroying the region's usefulness as a source of supplies for the Confederate armies. The Union troops arrived in Marianna on September 27, 1864. A short, brutal battle ensued, resulting in destruction of much of the town, the deaths of ten defenders and wounding of sixteen more, and the deaths of eight Union soldiers. The surprisingly staunch defense of Marianna checked the Union advance. The troops withdrew to Pensacola, seizing almost four dozen civilian captives from Jackson County, and followed by hundreds of self-emancipating slaves. Cox, *The Battle of Marianna, Florida*, 93.

13. The Union army accepted the surrender of Florida's Confederate government

and forces at Tallahassee and declared all slaves in Florida emancipated in mid-May 1865, more than one month after the surrender of General Lee's army at Appomattox. Richardson, *The Negro in the Reconstruction of Florida, 1876–1877*, 9.

14. Joseph W. Russ Sr. (1813–1883) was a prosperous Jackson County planter and political moderate. Adams's profile of Fortune described a member of the Russ family as Emanuel's "young master of the same age as himself." They "were reared together, and a strong affection . . . existed between them." Adams, "Timothy Thomas Fortune," 225. Joseph W. Russ, however, was twenty years older than Emanuel Fortune.

15. In his annual "Governor's Message" to the state assembly dated November 21, 1864, shortly after the Battle of Marianna, John Milton wrote that "[i]n this conflict the baseness, cruelty and perfidy of our foe have exceeded all precedent; they have developed a character so odious that death would be preferable to reunion with them." *A Journal of Proceedings of the House of Representatives of the General Assembly of the State of Florida at its Thirteenth Session* (1864). Milton affirmed his declared preference when he committed suicide at Sylvania, his Jackson County plantation, on April 1, 1865.

16. Fortune exaggerates the helplessness and passivity of the Jackson County black community. Several hundred Jackson County enslaved people emancipated themselves in late September 1864 when they followed Asboth's column on its retreat to Pensacola. Rita Dickens, *Marse Ned: The Story of an Old Southern Family* (New York: Exposition Press, 1958), 57–61. Some men in this group immediately enlisted in United States Colored Troops regiments. Twenty-five African Americans born in Jackson County can be identified on the rolls of sailors in the Civil War–era Union Navy. http://www.nps.gov/civilwar/soldiers-and-sailors-database.htm: accessed December 31, 2013.

17. In 1866, the African American population of Jackson County, Florida, exceeded five thousand, constituting about one-half of the county. C. M. Hamilton to T. W. Osborn, February 10, 1866, Records, Florida, BRF&AL. Jackson County was almost entirely rural, with only the village of Marianna and, to a much lesser degree, the satellite hamlets of Greenwood and Campbellton, containing any sort of concentrated population. Fortune's impression of Jackson County's small black population probably stems from his subsequent experience living in Jacksonville and Tallahassee, with larger black populations, and later his adulthood, when he resided in the urban centers of Washington, DC, and New York City.

18. The marriage certificate of Emanuel Fortune and Sarah J. Mires, dated June 5, 1866, can be found in the records of the Jackson County, Florida, courthouse.

19. The myth of the "Lost Cause" of the Confederacy emerged among southern veterans in the immediate wake of the war to rationalize the Confederacy's defeat as arising not from any battlefield inferiority but as a direct result of the crushing weight of northern industrial capacity and population advantage. The Lost Cause

myth evolved over time as its promotion became the preserve of the United Daughters of the Confederacy and the United Confederate Veterans. These groups laid the path that gradually led toward national empathy for a southern-oriented narrative of the Civil War's causes and Reconstruction's impact, with the corollary effect of reinforcing white belief in racial supremacy. For a discussion of the "Lost Cause" see David Blight, *Race and Reunion* (Cambridge: Harvard University Press, 2001), 255–90.

20. Freedmen's Bureau officer Charles M. Hamilton (1840–1875) reported the murder of Gilbert Walker, "a freedman of excellent character," by Hugh Parker, "of notorious reputation," on February 2, 1867. According to Hamilton, "Gilbert, engaged in hauling lumber, met a Mr. Bell driving an empty one ox cart in the public road, both gave way, but the road being narrow, and Gilbert heavily loaded, sufficient space to pass could not be given, and both stopped. Gilbert got down and held aside some bushes to permit Bell to pass—which he did. At this juncture Parker came up, *on foot*, and demanded of Gilbert why he did not turn out of the road. Gilbert replied that he did as far as he could. Parker retorted 'If you ever do that again I'll kill you'—and cursing him, added 'I might as well do it now'—and put a revolver to his breast and shot him—Gilbert expired in fifteen minutes. Efforts were, at the time, and have since been made to arrest the murderer, but he is still at large." C. M. Hamilton to E. C. Woodruff, February 4, 1867, Records, Florida, BRF&AL. The accused, Hugh Parker, was not a Jackson County resident and was thought to have escaped to Texas. Weinfeld, *The Jackson County War*, 29. Fortune is correct that, prior to this crime, murders in Jackson County were uncommon, rarely exceeding two per year. Two freedmen, however, had been slain in the two months preceding the Walker murder, one reportedly shot by planters who suspected the victim of stealing corn. C. M. Hamilton to E. C. Woodruff, December 31, 1866, Records, Florida, BRF&AL; Ethelred Philips to James J. Philips, Dec. 19, 1866, James John Philips papers, Manuscripts Department, Library of the University of North Carolina at Chapel Hill.

21. Fortune is confusing Gilbert Walker's murderer with other notorious Jackson County Regulators. Organized, secretive bands of whites, known variously as Regulators, Redeemers, Young Men's Democratic Clubs, or the Ku Klux Klan, had taken root in Florida by 1868 when most southern states were being readmitted to the Union under Republican administrations in accordance with the Congressional Reconstruction plan. Jackson County's Regulators were led by James P. Coker, a prominent merchant, and James F. McClellan, an attorney. Violence was perpetrated mostly by idle young Marianna men and by a few select hired assassins. US House *Report No. 22*, 112–13, 144, 147, 150. Weinfeld, *The Jackson County War*, 68–72.

22. With the exception of the bloody, one-day incursion in September 1864, Union troops never occupied Jackson County prior to the surrender of Florida's Confederate government and forces in mid-May 1865. Army commanders

considered Jackson County a strategic point and, beginning in July 1865, periodically dispatched officers and small details of troops to Marianna. These officers, however, did not interfere with relations between newly freed laborers and their former masters in more than a perfunctory manner. Plantation slavery continued in effect through the cotton harvest of late 1865. Inferring that their priorities included promoting a successful harvest in the fall and forestalling newly freed slaves from gathering in villages and towns, these army officers were complicit with the local planters' goal of pressuring black laborers to remain exactly where they had lived and to continue working the plantations. Dr. Ethelred Phillips of Marianna reported that these soldiers were "of great use to us in making the Negroes stay home and return when they leave." Ethelred Phillips to J. J. Philips, August 2, 1865. The few contracts entered into between planters and laborers in late 1865 provided compensation for labor from dawn to dusk only in the form of some clothing, housing, and food. The arrival of Charles M. Hamilton to establish the post of Freedmen's Bureau subassistant commissioner for Jackson and its surrounding counties in late January 1866 signaled the first serious attempt to impose contracts that remunerated laborers with wages or crops. Under Hamilton's assertive guidance, shaped by his sincere belief that the crop share system was advantageous to laborers in a cash-starved economy, the transition from slave-gangs working plantation lands to laborers operating in small, family-based units, was rapid. A few laborers worked for wages, but most contracted for compensation in the form of one-third of the crop they harvested plus equipment and food. William James Purman (1840–1928), Hamilton's boyhood friend from central Pennsylvania, received the appointment of Freedmen's Bureau civil agent for Jackson County in March 1866. Before long, Hamilton and Purman recognized the fundamental weakness in the crop share system. The Bureau agents were repeatedly compelled to intervene to protect laborers from planters who sought to promote indebtedness among the laborers or to defraud them outright. The inevitable outcome of laborers' indebtedness was to bind freedmen to the planters' land for successive years to pay off their obligations. Weinfeld, *The Jackson County War*, 25–26, 46–47. Some Jackson County freedmen, including Emanuel Fortune, established independent farming operations. T. Thomas Fortune recalled that his father "made it a point to raise all the food supplies he would require and then he would look after his cotton acreage. His farm was always worked up to its full capacity. His barns were always full of corn and oats and his smokehouse of meat, while there was a good herd of cows to feed the dairy and plenty of vegetables in the garden." *Dallas Morning News*, December 2, 1894. In reports to their supervisors, Hamilton and Purman complained of the social ostracism and open insults inflicted on them by the whites of Jackson County, with a few notable exceptions. Hamilton and Purman did not mention in their letters or reports consecrating marriages or distributing Bibles. W. J. Purman to E. C. Woodruff, February 28, 1867, Records, Florida, BRF&AL.

23. Corporal John Smith and Private Frank Davenport of Co. K of the 7th US Infantry were detailed as clerks to William J. Purman's office in early 1868. W. J. Purman, March 11, 1868, Records, Florida, BRF&AL.

24. The school for freedmen children had been established by US troops in 1865, but teachers were not commonly recruited from among soldiers. When Hamilton arrived in January 1866, he found Samuel G. Braman, a Union army veteran from Maine, teaching at the freedmen's school. Braman was harassed by local whites. C. M. Hamilton to T. W. Osborn, Feb. 28, 1866, Records, Florida, BRF&AL. Braman departed Jackson County in the summer of 1866 after a falling out with Hamilton and Purman. Braman's successors during the early Reconstruction years were Jackson County whites, including women. The teaching pool soon expanded: the 1870 census identified several black women in Jackson County who listed their occupation as teachers. Hamilton repeatedly wrote of his astonishment at the eagerness of the black children for learning and observed that they, "as a general thing, manifest greater interest in education than do the whites." C. M. Hamilton to J. L. McHenry, March 31, 1866, Records, Florida, BRF&AL.

25. The Florida legislature passed an act in 1849 for the establishment of common schools for white children between the ages of five and eighteen. Subsequent progress in public education was uneven and slow. In 1860, Jackson County reported five common schools supported by a combination of tuition and public funding, but fewer than one-quarter of Jackson County's school-age white children attended some kind of school. Prior to emancipation, blacks were barred from schools. Shofner, *Jackson County, Florida—A History*, 183–84. See Thomas Everette Cochran, *History of Public-School Education in Florida* (Lancaster, PA: Press of the New Era Printing Company, 1921), 22–33.

26. The picnic shooting on Tuesday, September 28, 1869, triggered the most horrific outburst of violence of the Jackson County War of 1869–1871. The intended target of the assassins was most likely Calvin Rogers, an African American elected Jackson County constable. Rogers had accompanied a group of black women and children to picnic grounds at a popular spring outside Marianna. The party was ambushed en route, resulting in the shooting death of one man and a two-year-old boy, and the wounding of Rogers. A search party failed to find the assailants. The following evening, elsewhere in Jackson County, two men, one white and one black, were shot and badly wounded. Violence then spun out of control. *House Report No. 22*, 78, 290. "Sergeant" Thomas Bond or Joseph Barnes were blamed for much of the violence of 1869 including, specifically, the Finlayson-Purman shooting. Fortune, like many others, confused Greenwood planter Thomas Barnes and his son Joseph with Jackson County farmer Thomas Bond. Joseph Barnes was affiliated with Jackson County's Regulators, but Thomas Bond was most likely the assassin who terrorized the black community. Weinfeld, *The Jackson County War*, 71–73, 83–84.

27. Fortune's memories of the picnic shooting and the subsequent events of the fall of 1869 are problematic. After receiving threats from Regulators, Emanuel Fortune fled Jackson County the previous spring in fear for his life and moved to Jacksonville. Fortune reported that his father had abandoned his property in Jackson County and it is hardly believable that Emanuel Fortune also left his twelve-year-old son behind. Fortune's description of certain events where he would not have been present, almost six decades after their occurrence, was probably shaped by his familiarity with the massive 1872 report issued by the Congressional Joint Select Committee to Inquire Into the Condition of Affairs in the Late Insurrectionary States. Volume XIII ("Miscellaneous and Florida") includes vivid accounts of the picnic shooting and ensuing violence in Jackson County and testimony by Emanuel Fortune. *House Report No. 22*, 78, 290. In 1884, Fortune wrote that "standing before the thirteen bulky volumes . . . my blood runs cold at the merciless chronicle of murder and outrage, of defiance, inhumanity and barbarity on the one hand, and usurpation and tyranny on the other." Fortune, *Black and White*, 60. In his 1886 essay, *The Negro in Politics*, Fortune remarked that when gazing at the volumes "a cold chill creeps over me." Alexander, *T. Thomas Fortune*, 38. Fortune refers specifically to volume 13, page 192 of the "Ku Klux Conspiracy" report in a note he appended to his 1886 poem, "Bartow Black."

28. Emanuel Fortune testified before the Congressional "KKK" Committee that white youths in Marianna stoned and mistreated African American children walking to school. *House Report No. 22*, 96.

29. Thomas Gautier, a Marianna merchant and owner of a leather and shoe shop, had two sons, Charles and Thomas Jr., close in age to Fortune. 1860 US Census, Jackson County, Florida; Shofner, *Jackson County*, 232.

30. The Russ plantation was located a few miles northwest of Marianna.

31. Patience Campbell was interviewed in 1936 by a Federal Writers' Project field worker and described her memories of growing up in slavery in Jackson County, Florida. Like Emanuel Fortune, Campbell's father, Arnold Merritt, practiced the trades of shoemaking and tanning. Campbell described the process of shoemaking: "after tanning and curing his hides by placing them in water with oak bark for several days and then exposing them to the sun to dry, [her father] would cut out the uppers and the soles after measuring the foot to be shod. There would be an inside sole as well as an outside sole tacked together by means of small tacks made of maple wood. Sewing was done on the shoes by means of flax thread." Works Progress Administration (WPA), *Slave Narratives Project*, vol. 3, Florida (Washington, DC: Government Printing Office, 1941), 59.

32. Under the Reconstruction plan imposed by Congress, elections for delegates to a Florida state constitutional convention were scheduled for November 1867. Most whites boycotted the referendum. Jackson County elected two whites and two blacks, all Republicans, including William J. Purman and Emanuel

Fortune. Emanuel Fortune described a voter registration visit he made with Hamilton to Walton County where the two men ended up in a dangerous melee with local whites. Weinfeld, *The Jackson County War*, 45–46; *House Report No. 22*, 98–99; Weinfeld, "Charles M. Hamilton," *FHQ*, 491–92. At the chaotic, tumultuous convention that convened in late January 1868, Fortune played a prominent role, siding with the "moderate" wing of the Republican Party. According to John Wallace, "but for [Fortune's] unalterable opposition as one of the colored delegates, it is doubtful whether the Purman-Osborn faction would have succeeded." John Wallace, *Carpetbag Rule in Florida,* 55.

33. Emanuel Fortune testified that in the months prior to his departure for Jacksonville in May 1869, Jackson County was in "such a state of lawlessness and outrage that I expected that my life was in danger at all times." *House Report No. 22*, 94.

34. Adams's account, predating "After War Times" by twenty-five years, contained a similarly vivid description of Emanuel Fortune's fortification of his home. According to Adams, T. Thomas Fortune rued "that the Ku Klux never stormed that fortress. They hung around the house at all hours of the night, but they never had the courage to attack it. They were cowards then as they are cowards now." Adams, "Timothy Thomas Fortune," 226.

35. On the evening of Friday, October 1, 1869, three days after the picnic shootings, James P. Coker and James F. McClellan, leaders of Jackson County's Regulators, stood on the veranda of the hotel in Marianna's main square with McClellan's teenage daughter, Maggie. Around 9 P.M., gunshots emanating from the darkness resulted in the death of Maggie and the wounding of her father. The next morning, white vigilantes seized control of Marianna. John Quincy Dickinson, "Memoranda of Occurrences relating to the assassinations in Jackson County September 28th 1869 & following," Kaplan Collection; *House Report No. 22*, 78, 290. The shooting of the McClellans was ascribed to black retaliation for the picnic shootings. The white community held Calvin Rogers accountable and he was tracked down and murdered early in 1870. Fortune paid tribute to Rogers in his 1886 poem, "Bartow Black."

36. The Fortune family had fled Jackson County in May 1869, months before the terrible events of the fall of 1869. Fortune is probably recalling the chaotic evening following the shooting of Dr. John L. Finlayson and William J. Purman the previous February. Purman testified that in the immediate wake of that ambush, a large group of armed blacks assembled with the intention of sacking Marianna in revenge for the shooting of their friends. Emanuel Fortune, closely aligned with Purman, was by his own admission "a leading man in politics" in Jackson County and might very likely have been approached by whites and asked to urge the group to disperse. In his own testimony, Purman took credit for averting further violence. *House Report No. 22*, 155. Emanuel Fortune recalled that he "would talk

very liberally" with his white antagonists and that "they generally respected me to my face." *House Report, No. 22*, 94.

37. Under ownership of the Baltzell family, the Marianna *Courier* was a fervently partisan Democratic Party organ that relentlessly attacked the state's Republican administration and reserved its most bitter venom to strike at Hamilton and Purman.

38. Horace Greeley (1811–1872): editor of the *New York Tribune* from which he ardently opposed slavery and promoted the Republican Party. Fortune is probably referring to Douglass's establishing a print shop to publish his abolitionist newspaper, the *North Star*, in Rochester, New York, in 1847.

39. Union soldiers burned St. Luke's Episcopal Church to flush out Confederates who had holed up there during the 1864 battle, and several defenders died in the fire. Cox, *The Battle of Marianna*, 66.

40. Apalachicola, Florida, was a small but thriving port located on the Gulf of Mexico coast, nearly one hundred miles from Marianna.

41. Patience Campbell also remembered the joys of Sunday biscuits during her Jackson County childhood when interviewed in 1936 by a Federal Writers' Project field worker. WPA *Slave Narratives*, vol. 3, 59.

42. Ebenezer Don Carlos Bassett (1833–1908): a prominent African American teacher and abolitionist in Philadelphia, became the first black appointed as a United States diplomat when the Grant administration named him minister to Haiti and the Dominican Republic in 1869.

43. Fortune is almost certainly thinking of Thomas Bond who gained notoriety as a suspected assassin affiliated with Jackson County's Regulators. Weinfeld, *The Jackson County War*, 71–73.

44. Hamilton left Marianna to move to Jacksonville in January 1868 after his term of service with the Freedmen's Bureau ended. He was elected to Congress the following May. In Jackson County's May 1868 election, Emanuel Fortune was elected to the state legislature and Purman to the state senate. Weinfeld, *The Jackson County War*, 49, 59. Purman spent very little time in Jackson County after being shot in early 1869. The school for freedmen children in Marinna may have closed periodically when no teachers were available, but appears to have stayed open regularly. Other Jackson County schools, however, closed often because of the scarcity of funds, teachers, and books, and threats of violence.

45. It is an exaggeration to describe the Finlaysons as the only loyalist family in Marianna. West Florida was known as a strongly Whig and Unionist region before and during the war with the reputation as a "citadel of whiggery." Even during Reconstruction, Hamilton and Purman succeeded in finding scattered white allies in Jackson County: John F. Barfield, Benjamin H. Neel, and James McMillan all won elections to the Florida legislature as Republicans; Rev. Jonathan W. Jenkins served as a voter registrar and, briefly, as county judge; Basheba Thomas held the

federally appointed position of postmistress for several years and insisted she had remained loyal during the Civil War. Dr. L. C. Armistead, a former state legislator, also served as a voter registrar in 1867 and was elected a Republican delegate to the 1868 state constitutional convention. Samuel Fleishman, a German-Jewish merchant who had lived in the region since the late 1840s, publicly allied himself with the Bureau agents. Fortune recalled working as a "store boy" for Fleishman and remarked that Fleishman had been resented by whites for obtaining "most of the Negro trade." Fortune was correct, however, in remembering the Finlaysons as the Marianna family most openly sympathetic to the Bureau officers. Dr. John L. Finlayson, the eldest son of a fairly prosperous, slave-owning planter, became close friends with Hamilton and Purman and aligned himself with the Republicans, attending a Florida Republican convention in 1867 and becoming an officer of the Jackson County Republican Party. Finlayson taught at a freedmen's night school for adults, accepted appointments as Bureau medical officer, Jackson County clerk of court, and as acting Bureau agent during Purman's frequent absences from Marianna. Even more remarkably, Dr. Finlayson's sisters, Martha Mary and Leadora, married Hamilton and Purman, respectively. The Hamilton wedding took place in March 1868, one month after John L. Finlayson's murder, and the Purman wedding three years later. *New York Age*, August 21, 1913; Daniel R. Weinfeld, "Samuel Fleishman: Tragedy in Reconstruction-Era Florida," *Southern Jewish History* 8 (2005), 44; Weinfeld, *The Jackson County War*, 2, 23–24, 39.

46. On February 26, 1869, around 10 P.M., Finlayson and Purman were walking back from a concert given by the local garrison when a hidden assailant fired a load of buckshot at them. As Fortune accurately recalled, Finlayson, shot in the temple, fell dead, and Purman, struck in the neck, was severely wounded. J. Q. Dickinson, "A Letter from Florida," in *Rutland* (VT) *Daily Herald*, April 15, 1869; *House Report, No. 22*, 99.

47. In the two months following the Finlayson-Purman shooting, several more attacks took place in Jackson County, including at least four murders. John Q. Dickinson, Purman's successor as Freedmen's Bureau agent, and, later, Finlayson's replacement as Jackson County clerk of court, wrote to his father in Vermont that "every night or two some one, generally a good Republican is shot at from some ambush but never in the daylight." J. Q. Dickinson to Isaac Dickinson, April 11, 1869, John Q. Dickinson Collection, Bailey/Howe Library, University of Vermont; *Tallahassee Weekly Floridian*, April 27, 1869.

48. In his November 1871 testimony before the congressional committee that convened in Jacksonville, Emanuel Fortune dated his departure from Jackson County as May 1869. The Florida legislature held a brief, second "special" session in June, although the Senate Journal does not mention appointment of a page. Timothy was appointed senate page in 1870 and again in 1871. He was not appointed to the 1872 session. *A Journal of the Proceedings of the Senate of the State of*

Florida, 1869, 1870, 1871, 1872. Elsewhere, Fortune admitted that his selection as page was a result of his father's influence. Alexander, *T. Thomas Fortune*, 49.

49. In the eyes of young Tim Fortune, Jacksonville, with a population of more than 5,000, and Tallahassee with 2,000 residents, were large cities in 1869, compared to Marianna which claimed fewer than 1,000 people. Brown, *Florida's Black Public Officials*, 44.

50. William G. Steward (1839–1911), one of the founders of the African Methodist Episcopal Church in Florida, served as chaplain of the Florida state legislature for several sessions and held a number of public offices, including one term in the state legislature and many years as Tallahassee's postmaster. Brown, *Florida's Black Public Officials*, 4, 128. Theophilus G. Steward (1843–1924) was also ordained in the African Methodist Episcopal Church and active in Reconstruction-era politics in Georgia. In addition to teaching and writing, Steward spent sixteen years as chaplain of the 25th US Colored Infantry regiment. William Seraile, "Theophilus G Steward, Intellectual Chaplain, 25th US Colored Infantry," *Nebraska History* 66 (1985): 272–93.

51. Jonathan C. Gibbs (1827–1874), a Dartmouth College graduate and minister, was acclaimed as one of the most talented and intelligent public officials in Florida during the Reconstruction period. If Fortune's estimation of the very accomplished Gibbs—the first African American to hold statewide office in Florida—seems somewhat muted, the cause would be the bitter political rivalry between Gibbs and Fortune's good friend and patron, William J. Purman. The Gibbs-Purman antagonism dated back to the divisive 1868 Florida state constitutional convention, when Purman's ruthless tactics helped secure the convention floor for the mostly white "moderate" Republicans at the expense of "radicals" with whom Gibbs and most black delegates were aligned (Emanuel Fortune was one of four black delegates to join the moderates). Their enmity became more vindictive over time. In addition to the achievements that Fortune listed, Thomas Van Renssalaer Gibbs (1855–1898) served two terms in the Florida state legislature and was a delegate to the state's 1885 constitutional convention. The State Normal College for Colored Students was the predecessor of Florida A&M University. Brown, 92; Larry E. Rivers and Canter Brown Jr., "A Monument to the Progress of the Race: The Intellectual and Political Origins of the Florida Agricultural and Mechanical University, 1865–1887," *Florida Historical Quarterly* (Summer 2006): 2; on Jonathan C. Gibbs, see Learotha Williams, "'A Wider Field of Usefulness': The Life and Times of Jonathan Clarkson Gibbs, c. 1828–1874" (PhD dissertation, Florida State University, 2003). After an adventurous decade in California and British Columbia (where he was elected to the city council), Mifflin W. Gibbs (1823–1915) attended Oberlin College and served as a municipal judge in Little Rock, AR, for two years during Reconstruction. For the remainder of his long life, Gibbs was a leader of the Arkansas black community, a businessman, and an active

member of the Republican Party. M. W. Gibbs reciprocated Fortune's regard as evidenced by the caption under a photo of Fortune included in Gibbs's autobiography that described Fortune as: "Polished and Able . . . The Most Aggressive and Trenchant Writer of the Negro Press." Mifflin Wistar Gibbs, *Shadow and Light An Autobiography with Reminiscences of the Last and Present Century* (Washington, DC, 1902), 210.

52. The Napiers of Nashville and the Langstons of Ohio were closely entwined families, with pairs of siblings marrying. The Napiers also maintained a life-long, close relationship with Fortune's longtime associate, Booker T. Washington. James Carroll Napier (1845–1940) had a long career as a prominent attorney, banker, and public figure in Nashville. For more about the Napier family, see Bobby L. Lovett, *The African American History of Nashville, Tennessee, 1790–1930: Elites and Dilemmas* (Fayetteville: University of Arkansas Press, 1999). John Mercer Langston (1829–1897) graduated from Oberlin College and was admitted to the Ohio bar. In addition to founding and serving as dean of Howard University's Law Department, Langston held a number of distinguished political, diplomatic, and academic positions. He was a Republican candidate for Congress from Virginia in 1888 and took his seat in the House after successfully challenging the initial award of the election to his Democratic opponent, thereby becoming the first black Congressman from Virginia. After Langston's death, Fortune wrote of his first encounter with Langston on the Howard campus: "I had never seen a man of my race who approached Mr. Langston in polish and graces of manner, in faultlessness of dress, and in consciousness of superiority to all things around him, and, I may add, I have never seen one since." Fortune remarked that upon the death of Frederick Douglass, Langston "easily became the greatest man of his race." New York *Sun*, Nov. 21, 1897. Langston had resigned from the Howard University in July 1875 "after being passed over as permanent university president" but joined the law school faculty. Susan D. Carle, "The Lawyer's Role in a Contemporary Democracy, Promoting Social Change and Political Values, Debunking the Myth of Civil Rights Liberalism: Visions of Racial Justice in the Thought of T. Thomas Fortune, 1880–1890," *Fordham Law Review*, vol. 77, issue 4 (2009), 1490.

53. J. C. Napier's younger brother, Henry Alonzo Napier (1851–1882), Fortune's friend, was an early African American cadet at West Point. Napier's arrival at the military academy in June 1871 was considered the "greatest sensation of the season." A correspondent of the *Sentinel* shared Fortune's admiration of Napier, describing him as "dignified, complaisant, ready spoken, and quite charming as a conversationalist. He is said to be very patient and even-tempered, but not at all likely to suffer being trampled on unjustly." Tallahassee *Sentinel*, June 10, 1871. Napier was dismissed from the academy the following June, ostensibly for failing exams in math and French, but some believed that he was the victim of the racially motivated hazing from other cadets (including Frederick Dent Grant, son

of President Grant) that plagued other early black cadets, including James Webster Smith and Fortune's friend, Thomas V. Gibbs. *New York Sun*, Oct. 14, 1894. General Oliver O. Howard, Commissioner of the Freedmen's Bureau, investigated Napier's plight at the Academy and concluded that "no barbarian could torture a captive so as to wound him in spirit more keenly than other young fellows have done to Napier simply because it is in their power." William S. McFeely, *Grant: A Biography* (New York: W. W. Norton & Co., 1981), 379.

54. Charles H. Pearce (1820–1887), born free in Maryland, was an AME minister dispatched to Florida in early 1866 to organize and lead the church. Pearce was elected a delegate to the 1868 Florida Constitutional Convention and represented Leon County in the state senate for most of the Reconstruction era. He also held a number of appointed positions in Leon County. Born in Gadsden County, Florida, Robert Meacham (1835–1902), served as an AME and AME Zion minister. He was a delegate to the 1868 Constitutional Convention and represented Jefferson County in the Florida senate throughout the entire Reconstruction era. William Bradwell (1822–1887) was an AME minister and 1868 Constitutional Convention delegate. He represented Duval County (Jacksonville) in the Florida senate. These three men were the only African Americans elected to Florida's twenty-four member senate in 1868. Blacks held seventeen seats in the fifty-three member Florida legislature. Emanuel Fortune was one of Jackson County's three legislators in the 1868–1870 sessions. Frederick Hill (1833–1893) was a delegate to the 1868 Constitutional Convention before representing Gadsden County in the Florida legislature and then senate. Alfred Brown Osgood (1843–1911), an AME minister, was elected from Madison County to the legislature and later the senate. John Robert Scott Sr. (1840–1879), another AME minister, represented Duval County in the legislature and received the federal appointment of collector of the Port of Jacksonville. Henry S. Harmon (1839–1889) (whose name Fortune mistakes as "Harry"), a Pennsylvania-born US Colored Troops veteran and Florida's first African American attorney, served in the Florida legislature from Alachua County. Brown, *Florida's Black Public Officials*, 13, 76, 95, 97, 109–110, 113–115, 123,146–48; Rivers and Brown, "A Monument to the Progress of the Race," *FHQ*, 17; on Charles H. Pearce, see Dorothy Dodd, "Bishop Pearce and the Reconstruction of Leon County, " *Apalachee* (1946), 5–12; on Robert Meacham, see Brown Jr., "'Where Are Now the Hopes I Cherished?" *FHQ*, 1–36; on Henry S. Harmon, see Young, "Henry S. Harmon," *FHQ*, 177–96. Fortune became a harsh critic of the carpetbagger-led Reconstruction-era governments. In *The Negro in Politics*, Fortune wrote that some black politicians during Reconstruction were "capable and honest and remained uncontaminated by the fetid atmosphere they breathed." The majority, however, "succumbed to the pernicious teachings and corrupt practices of their white associates and masters." Alexander, *T. Thomas Fortune*, 40.

55. "General Butler of Walton county" was John W. Butler (1830–1881) of

Santa Rosa County, located two Panhandle counties west of Walton. Butler, a native of Massachusetts, was indeed "bulky," reportedly standing 6'3" and weighing over three hundred pounds. His title came from his appointment as major general of the Florida state militia. He was a Santa Rosa County delegate to the 1868 Constitutional Convention, elected to the state legislature, and afterward appointed sheriff. Nathan Woolsey, "Butler Was First Republican Sheriff," *Santa Rosa Press Gazette*, November 16, 1992.

56. Charles Henry Walton (1834–1877) arrived in Florida in 1867 and held the position of state printer for most of the Reconstruction era. Walton owned and edited the Tallahassee *Sentinel* newspaper which, as the organ of the state's Republican administration, printed laws and the journal of legislative sessions.

57. Salvador T. Pons (1835–1890) was elected to the Florida legislature from Escambia County. He also served as a councilman, mayor, and clerk in Pensacola. Josiah T. Walls (1842–1905), a US Colored Troops veteran, was elected as a delegate to the 1868 Constitutional Convention from Alachua County. After representing Alachua County in the legislature and senate, Walls became the first African American from Florida sent to the United States Congress, where he was elected three times (although twice unseated in contested elections). Brown, *Florida's Black Public Officials*, 116, 135–36; for Josiah T. Walls see D. Peter Klingman, *Josiah Walls*. Klingman does not mention Fortune's serving as Walls's secretary. If Fortune did work for Walls, it was probably in very late 1875 or early 1876 soon after Fortune arrived in Washington, DC. John Wallace described Emanuel Fortune as a "forcible debater" and similarly attested to Emanuel Fortune's incorruptible reputation: "whenever he believed he was right, neither money nor promises could move him from his position." Wallace, *Carpetbag Rule*, 55. Reflecting on his father's experience in Tallahassee, T. Thomas Fortune wrote that Emanuel Fortune "came out of that cesspool of duplicity, cunning and corruption an honest man, wiser than when he went into it." Alexander, *T. Thomas Fortune*, 49. On a visit to Tallahassee years later, Fortune lamented that he could find no trace or memory of the personalities who loomed larger-than-life in his youthful mind. *New York Sun*, December 29, 1895. Fortune was much kinder to carpetbaggers in "After War Times" than in earlier writings, such as the 1886 pamphlet, "The Negro in Politics," where he denounced their "mercenary character" and accused them of deceiving blacks and selling "them out to the enemy for a paltry mess of pottage." He excluded from such criticism "some of the carpet-bagger politicians of Florida, whom I knew personally," naming Purman, Hamilton, and Dickinson. Alexander, *T. Thomas Fortune*, 49.

58. Governor Ossian Hart appointed Jonathan C. Gibbs superintendent of public instruction in 1873. Rivers and Brown, "A Monument to the Progress of the Race," *FHQ*, 12–16; on Governor Hart's appointment of Jonathan C. Gibbs, see Brown, *Ossian Bingley Hart*, 273. Fortune is mistaken about the fate of the

Republican-enacted 1868 state constitution: in 1886 Florida voters approved a new constitution drafted by Democrats that greatly reduced the expansive powers of appointment granted the governor under the 1868 constitution, enacted clauses crafted to reduce the voting strength of counties with large black populations, authorized segregated schooling, and authorized a poll tax. Williamson, *Florida Politics in the Gilded Age*, 137–43. Fortune came to deeply resent the Republican Party for its abandonment of southern blacks ensuing from the "shameful bargain" that settled the 1876 presidential election dispute. Fortune's bitterness, however, caused him to accept too readily allegations of financial incompetence on the part of Reconstruction-era southern Republican state governments, at least in his native Florida. Florida's government, under the Republican administration of Governor Ossian Hart, set the state on a path of fiscal responsibility and stability. Shofner, *Nor Is It Over Yet*, 291–92. Brown, *Ossian Bingley Hart*, 280–81, 292. For Fortune's anger toward the Republican Party for its "base ingratitude, subterfuge and hypocrisy to its black partisan allies," see Fortune, *Black and White*, 59–60, 77; and Alexander, *T. Thomas Fortune*, 16, 21–22, 24, 41–42, 78, 94, 107.

59. The tombstone inscribed "Sarah Jane wife of E. Fortune Sr." in Jacksonville's Old City Cemetery lists a date of birth of July 4, 1838, and a date of death of Jan. 24, 1871, indicating that at the time of her death, Sarah Fortune was thirty-two years old and her son, Timothy, fourteen.

60. Fortune's four younger siblings were Martha (1858–?), Florence (1861–?), Emanuel Jr. (1862–1890), and Mary (1867–?). Emanuel Fortune Sr. married Catherine E. Richard (1853–1895) on December 23, 1872, in Duval County.

61. According to two biographical sketches predating the "After War Times" articles by more than forty years, Fortune received the federal patronage appointment as mail route agent ("through the kindly offices of Hon. W. J. Purman") in 1875 when he was eighteen years old. *New York Freeman*, February 27, 1886; W. J. Simmons, *Men of Mark* (Cleveland, 1887), 786. Adams's account from 1902 and a biographical profile by Booker T. Washington from 1907, however, date the mail route agency appointment back to 1874. Adams, "Timothy Thomas Fortune," 226; Booker T. Washington, *The Negro in Business*, Boston Hertel, Jenkins & Co. 1907, 179. Biographer Emma Lou Thornbrough accepts the "After War Times" dates. Thornbrough, *T. Thomas Fortune*, 23–24. After visiting Purman in Boston in 1891, Fortune described Purman as "the best friend I ever had" and "as good a friend to me to day as he was when he dictated the course of Florida politics." *New York Age*, June 30, 1891. The Jacksonville, Pensacola and Mobile Railroad Company was formed out of the remnants of failed Florida railroads under murky circumstances and was embroiled in scandal and litigation soon after its founding in 1869. The company failed to extend the railroad west past Chattahoochee as authorized by its state charter, did not pay interest on bonds, and was seized by the state before collapsing into bankruptcy. For Florida railroads during the Reconstruction era and

the Swepson-Littlefield fraud, see Shofner, *Nor Is It over Yet,* 243–57; Gregg M. Turner, *A Journey into Florida Railroad History* (Gainvesville: University of Florida Press, 2008), 90–103.

62. The Atlantic and Gulf Railroad, originating in Savannah, Georgia, was extended briefly during the Civil War to Live Oak, Florida, and the connection was completed in late 1866, allowing direct travel from Tallahassee to Savannah. Shofner, *Nor Is It over Yet,* 112–13.

63. "Walker" is possibly Robert Walker—general superintendant of the Jacksonville, Pensacola and Mobile Railroad who became the court appointed receiver of the troubled company in April 1874. C. J. French was a Post Office Department superintendant of the Railway Mail Service (RMS) for the South and later was named general manager of the American Bell Co.

64. Colonel John Jackson Dickison (1816–1902) (whose name Fortune mistakes as "Dickinson") was the preeminent Confederate soldier active in Florida during the Civil War. He led his small cavalry unit on a series of successful guerrilla raids repelling Union army incursions. During Reconstruction, Dickison was active in voter intimidation and resistance to Florida's Republican government. He has been accused of organizing the 1868 theft and destruction of hundreds of rifles procured by Governor Reed and intended for the state's militia. Dickison was appointed Florida's Adjutant General in 1877 and later major general of the state militia. Jerrell H. Shofner, *Nor Is It over Yet,* 331; Vince Murray, "Captain J. J. Dickison: Marion County's Civil War Hero," in www.ocala.com, January 1, 2003. Dickison's sons John J. Jr. and Robert had reputations for violence. Charles A. Hentz, *The Autobiography of Dr. C. A. Hentz, Florida and North Carolina, 1827–1894,* Vol. II, Originals on File in the Southern Historical Collection, University of North Carolina Library, Chapel Hill. Robert L. Dickison died in 1878, and John Jr. was lynched in 1881 after being accused of attempted murder. *Fenandina Florida Mirror,* Aug. 8, 1881.

65. Before the Civil War, Edward S. Hopkins (1810–1887) was a state senator and then Constitutional Union Party candidate for governor of Florida in 1860. His poor performance as a colonel of a Forida regiment in the Confederate army resulted in rejection by his troops during the election of officers in the spring of 1862. Hopkins was elected Jacksonville's mayor from 1868 to 1870. Although a Democrat, he allied with more moderate Republicans but was defeated by the Republican candidate in 1871. Bruce S. Allardice, *Confederate Colonels: A Biographical Register,* (Columbia: University of Missouri Press, 2008), 202; Thomas Frederick Davis, *History of Jacksonville, Florida and Vicinity: 1513 to 1924* (St. Augustine, FL: Florida Historical Society, 1925, reprint ed. Gainesville: University of Florida Press, 1964), 294–95.

66. In "After War Times," Fortune glosses over the years he lived in Jacksonville

beginning in mid-1869. According to a much earlier biographical profile, composed when Fortune was not yet thirty years old, Fortune, soon after settling in Jacksonville, apprenticed in the office of the Jacksonville *Daily Florida Union,* where he learned typesetting. After a change in management at the newspaper, Fortune attended for two years the Stanton Normal School, operated by the American Missionary Association, Duval County, and the Freedmen's Bureau. According to the same account, he then worked as an office boy and "letter stamper and paper clerk" in the Jacksonville post office until his appointment in 1875 as a mail route agent. *New York Freeman*, February 27, 1886. See also *Norfolk Journal and Guide,* January 12, 1924; Simmons, *Men of Mark*, 786; Penn, *The African American Press and Its Editors*, 133–34; Joe M. Richardson, "Christian Abolitionism: The American Missionary Association and the Florida Negro," *The Journal of Negro Education*, 40 (Winter 1971), 41–42. Because the Florida legislature was typically in session only during January, part of February, and perhaps a week or two over the summer for a special session, this information accounts for much of Fortune's activities during the early 1870s. Fortune's obtaining employment in the post office may be attributed to Charles M. Hamilton's temporary appointment as Jacksonville postmaster for the second half of 1871.

67. Emanuel Fortune had a long and distinguished career in Jacksonville public affairs, which included serving as city marshal, county commissioner of Duval County, and a member of the city's board of health. He was a delegate to the Republican National Convention in 1876 and attended later conventions as an alternate and guest. After arriving in Jacksonville, Emanuel Fortune continued his practice of successfully forming cross-party alliances with white reformers. In 1887, for example, Fortune was elected to the Jacksonville city council from the white-dominated third district. Emanuel Fortune died in Jacksonville on January 27, 1897. *Cleveland Gazette*, February 6, 1897; *New York Sun*, January 28, 1897; Edward N. Akin, "Blacks in Jacksonville Politics, 1887–1907," *Florida Historical Quarterly* 53 (Oct. 1974), 125, 127, 131.

68. William W. Sampson (1821–1888), an AME minister, was a justice of the peace and Jacksonville town councilman during the 1870s. Brown, *Florida's Black Public Officials,* 122–23.

69. Fortune's dismissive opinion of Joseph E. Lee (1849–1920) was not universally shared. Ironically, Lee came to Florida as another protégé of Fortune's own patron, William J. Purman. Lee served many years in public service in Florida, including three years in the state legislature and long stints as US collector at the Port of Jacksonville, and as the US Collector of Internal Revenue for Florida. Brown, *Florida Black Public Officials*, 103–4. Rivers and Brown, "A Monument to the Progress of the Race," *FHQ,* 20–1; on Joseph E. Lee, see Gary B. Goodwin, "Joseph E. Lee of Jacksonville, 1880–1920" (master's thesis, Florida State University,

1996). In 1880, Emanuel Fortune joined with white reformers to support Jonathan C. Greeley's failed attempt to unseat Joseph E. Lee from the state senate. Akin, "Blacks in Jacksonville Politics," *FHQ*, 125. Emanuel Fortune again aligned with white reformers, including former governor Harrison Reed and former congressman Horatio Bisbee Jr., in another attempt in 1896 at ending Lee's domination of the state Republican Party and control over federal patronage. *New York Sun,* Feb. 23, 1896.

70. Perry Carson, known as the "tall black oak" and "the black boss" of Washington, was an influential figure in District of Columbia politics for decades, winning several party primaries to represent District of Columbia Republicans at national conventions. James H. Whyte, *The Uncivil War: Washington During the Reconstruction, 1865–1878* (New York: Twayne Publishers, 1958), 97; Washington *Post,* January 21, 1896, November 1, 1909.

71. Fortune's chronology continues to be vague. He enrolled in the Model School of the Normal Department at Howard University upon first arriving in Washington, DC in late 1875 or early 1876. *Catalogue of the Officers and Students of Howard University from June 1874 to February 1876*, (Washington, DC: O. H. Reed, 1876), 7. According to two accounts written much earlier than "After War Times," Fortune's employment as customs inspector lasted from mid-1876 through the end of that year. *New York Freeman*, February 27, 1886; Simmons, *Men of Mark*, 786. A later biographical profile, however, dated his holding this position back to 1875. Adams, "Timothy Thomas Fortune," 226. William D. Nolen was appointed Collector of Customs for the District of Delaware, Port of Wilmington, in April 1869. Nolen's son, Franklin, held the posts of deputy collector and inspector. Fortune probably took satisfaction from William Nolen's removal from office in late April 1876. Nolen was tried and convicted for embezzlement in November 1876, but pardoned by President Grant upon solicitation by "many of the most respectable citizens of Delaware." John Y. Simon, ed., *The Papers of Ulysses S. Grant, Volume 26: 1875*, (Carbondale, IL: Southern Illinois University Press, 2003), 219. Washington, DC, *Evening Star*, Nov. 29, 1876.

72. Edwina B. Kruse (1848–1930) helped establish schools for African American children in Delaware after the Civil War and served as principal of the Howard School—the only secondary school for African Americans in Delaware—into the 1920s.

73. The Delaware state legislature passed a law providing for racially separate public accommodations in 1875, prior to Fortune's arrival in the state. Two years earlier, the Democratic-controlled legislature enacted a poll tax and associated legislation that had the intended effect of disenfranchising blacks and facilitating Democratic one-party control of the state. Harold B. Hancock, "The Status of the Negro in Delaware after the Civil War, 1865–1875," *Delaware History*, vol. XIII, No. 1 (April 1968), 62, 64–65; Amy M. Hiller, "The Disenfranchisement of

Delaware Negroes in the Late Nineteenth Century," *Delaware History*, vol. XIII, No. 2 (October 1968), 124, 142–45.

74. Dr. Isaac H. Knowles established the *Breakwater Light*, later the *Delaware Pilot*, as a Republican newspaper in Lewes, Delaware, in 1871. Knowles and his son, Horace Greeley Knowles, were pillars of the Republican Party in Delaware for decades. George Derby and James T. White, *The National Cyclopaedia of American Biography, Volume XIV* (New York: James T. White Co., 1910), 487.

75. Fortune either intended to refer to the election of 1876 or is remembering events he witnessed in Jacksonville in 1872. Delaware voters gave their three electoral college votes to Democratic presidential candidate Samuel B. Tilden in the disputed 1876 election.

76. William Shakespeare, *Hamlet*, V, ii.

77. The following account seems to refer to Fortune's initial enrollment in Howard's Normal Department sometime during the 1875–1876 academic year. He entered Howard's Law Department during 1877–1878.

78. It is unclear why Fortune decided in "After War Times" to downplay his two years at the Stanton Institute school in Jacksonville (see note 66, above). While at Stanton, he declined an offer of a scholarship to attend Atlanta University because he objected to the condition that he study to become "a preacher or a teacher." Alexander, *T. Thomas Fortune*, 175–76. Howard University's three-year Preparatory Department program was intended to prepare students "for admission to any college course," including Howard's four-year College Department. The Normal Department's three-year program was designed to train teachers. Fortune initially entered Howard's Model School, which was administered by the Normal Department. Admission to the Model School required passing examinations in "Arithmetic (through long division), Reading, Spelling (common words of two syllables), and Elements of Geography." The Model School curriculum was intended to lead to admission to either the Normal or Preparatory Departments. Model School courses were taught by Normal Department students. *Catalogue of the Officers and Students of Howard University from June 1874 to February 1876*, 18–21.

79. James Monroe Gregory (1849–1915) studied at Oberlin and graduated from Howard University in 1872. He was appointed professor of Latin in 1875 and taught at Howard for two decades, which included serving as college dean during Fortune's years of attendance. Gregory became the principal of the Bordentown Industrial and Manual Training School in New Jersey in 1897. Simmons, *Men of Mark*, 631–41; Lois Brown, *Encyclopedia of the Harlem Literary Renaissance* (New York: Facts on File, Inc., 2006), 201. Thomas Robinson was dean of the Normal Department and college for several years during the 1870s and 1880s and taught science and chemistry. Martha Bailey Briggs (1838–1889) taught in public schools before joining Howard's Normal Department in 1873, where she was principal from 1883 until her death. Rayford W. Logan, *Howard University, The First*

Hundred Years 1967–1967 (New York: Howard University, 1968), 38–39, 57; Jessie Carney Smith, ed., *Notable Black Women, Book II* (Detroit: Gale Research Inc., 1996), 54–55.

80. George W. Mitchell received a law degree from Howard and taught classical languages and political economy until 1875. Logan, *Howard University*, 39.

81. Frederick Douglass purchased his Anacostia home in 1877 and moved there the following year. The house is preserved as the Frederick Douglass National Historic Site.

82. Fortune wrote that he chose to live off campus while attending Howard University because he objected to the strict religious requirements of the dormitory. Alexander, *T. Thomas Fortune*, 175.

83. Sumner I. Kimball (1834–1923), a lawyer from Maine, is credited with overhauling the Revenue Marine Division, which together with the US Life-Saving Service, also administered by Kimball, merged to form the modern US Coast Guard. http://www.uscg.mil/History/faqs/BIO_Sumner_Kimball.html.

84. Fortune was one of six students enrolled in Howard's Law Department for the 1877–1878 term. "Howard's law department operated as a part-time night program designed to be completed in two years." Carle, "Visions of Racial Justice in the Thought of T. Thomas Fortune, 1880–1890," *Fordham Law Review*, 1490. Applicants to the Law Department were required to "be well grounded in the common English branches, in rhetoric, and in elementary natural science" and have graduated college or passed examinations in "algebra, geometry, Latin, logic, mental science." Evidently, Fortune's level of academic achievement had progressed far since his entry in the Model School two years earlier. *Catalogue of the Officers and Students of Howard University from March 1876 to March 1878* (Washington, DC: W. M. Stuart, 1878) 8, 20–21. A biographical profile published only three years prior to "After War Times" stated that Fortune had entered the Law Department and read law for a year at Howard while working at the *People's Advocate*. *Norfolk Journal and Guide*, January 12, 1924.

85. John W. Cromwell (1846–1927), an attorney and educator, published the *People's Advocate*, a Washington weekly newspaper, from 1876 to 1884. An early graduate of Howard University Law School, Robert Peel Brooks (1857–1883) established a law practice and edited a newspaper in Richmond, Virginia. Richard T. Greener (1844–1922), the first African American graduate of Harvard College, was a diplomat, educator, and attorney. Greener taught at Howard's Law Department at the time Fortune was enrolled. See Michael R. Mounter, "Richard Theodore Greener: The Idealist, Statesman, Scholar, and South Carolinian" (PhD dissertation, University of South Carolina, 2002). Lewis H. Douglass (1840–1908), the son of Frederick Douglass, served as sergeant major in the 54th Massachusetts—the celebrated US Colored Troops regiment depicted in the movie *Glory*. Douglass held various public positions and was a District of Columbia

businessman. Charles N. Otey (1851–?) graduated from Howard and was a newspaper editor and educator.

86. Fortune was adamant that there "were no elements of a preacher or teacher in my makeup." Alexander, *T. Thomas Fortune*, 175–76. Fortune married Charlotte (Carrie) C. Smiley (1857–1940) of Jacksonville, Florida, on Feb. 21, 1878, in the District of Columbia. "District of Columbia Marriages, 1811–1950" index and images, *FamilySearch* (https://familysearch.org/pal:/MM9.1.1/XLSV-Z92: accessed 04 Mar 2013). Two of their children lived to adulthood: Jessie Bowser, an educator who settled in Sag Harbor, New York, and Dr. Frederick W. Fortune, chief of surgery at Mercy Hospital in Philadelphia. *New York Age*, June 5, 1937. Purman's defeat in his bid for reelection in 1876 and the subsequent loss of this patronage source, combined with financial problems at the *People's Advocate*, eventually forced the Fortunes to leave Washington and move back to Florida. Thornbrough, *T. Thomas Fortune*, 32, 97–99. Washington, DC. *Bee*, August 25, 1883. For a description of the Fortunes' marriage told by their granddaughter, Elizabeth Bowser, see Nina Tobier, ed., *Voices of Sag Harbor: A Village Remembered* (Sag Harbor, NY: Harbor Electronic Publishing, 2007), 39–44.

87. When considering Fortune's law school matriculation, marriage date, and his memories of Frederick Douglass at Anacostia, the Fortunes must have remained in Washington well into 1878. Adams, "Timothy Thomas Fortune," 226; *New York Freeman*, February 27, 1886; *Norfolk Journal and Guide*, January 12, 1924. Fortune arrived in New York to work with William Walter Sampson, a friend from Jacksonville, as a compositor and typesetter in late 1879 or early 1880. *New York Sun*, April 16, 1880. Frederick G. Detweiler, *The Negro Press in the United States* (Chicago: University of Chicago Press, 1922), 55–56; Penn, *The Afro-American Press and Its Editors*, 134. Fortune either briefly returned to Florida or left his young family behind as he sought reliable employment in New York. The 1880 Census lists "Tim," Carrie, and two infants (each of whom would die shortly) living in the home of Emanuel Fortune in Jacksonville. Elizabeth F. Gibbs, widow of Jonathan C. Gibbs, also resided with the Fortune family. 1880 US Census, Duval County, Florida.

Afterword

1. Thornbrough, *T. Thomas Fortune*; Emma Lou Thornbrough, "T. Thomas Fortune: Militant Editor in the Age of Accommodation," in John Hope Franklin and August Meier, eds., *Black Leaders of the Twentieth Century* (Urbana: University of Illinois Press, 1982), 19–37.

2. Susan D. Carle, "The Lawyer's Role in a Contemporary Democracy, Promoting Social Change and Political Values, Debunking the Myth of Civil Rights Liberalism: Visions of Racial Justice in the Thoughts of T. Thomas Fortune,

1880–1890," *Fordham Law Review* 77 (2009): 1484.

3. Ibid.

4. "Status of the Race: Mr. Fortune Before the United States Senate Committee on Education and Labor," *New York Globe*, September 22, 1883.

5. Carle, *Fordham Law Review*, 1508–1517.

6. T. Thomas Fortune, *Black and White*, 126.

7. Jacqueline Jones Royster, ed. *Southern Horrors and Other Writings: The Anti-Lynching Campaign of Ida B. Wells, 1892–1900* (Boston, 1997), 13; Alfreda M. Dunster, *Crusade for Justice: The Autobiography of Ida B. Wells* (Chicago: University of Chicago Press, 1970); Mia Bay, *To Tell the Truth Freely: The Life of Ida B. Wells* (New York: Hill and Wang , 2009).

8. Fortune, *Black and White*, 81.

9. Alexander, *T. Thomas Fortune*, xx.

10. Thornbrough, *T. Thomas Fortune*; Louis R. Harlan, *Booker T. Washington: The Wizard of Tuskegee, 1901–1915* (New York: Oxford University Press , 1983).

11. Alexander, *T. Thomas Fortune*, xxvii–xxiv.

Bibliography

Books and Articles

Adams, Cyrus Fields. "Timothy Thomas Fortune. Journalist, Author, Lecturer, Agitator." *The Colored American Magazine* IV (Jan. and Feb. 1902): 224–229.

Akin, Edward N., "Blacks in Jacksonville Politics, 1887–1907," *Florida Historical Quarterly* 53 (Oct. 1974), 123–45.

Alexander, Shawn L. *T. Thomas Fortune, the Afro-American Agitator.* Gainesville: University Press of Florida. 2008.

Allardice, Bruce S. *Confederate Colonels: A Biographical Register.* Columbia, Missouri: University of Missouri Press, 2008.

Baptist, Edward D. *Creating an Old South; Middle Florida's Plantation Frontier Before the Civil War.* Chapel Hill: University of North Carolina Press, 2002.

Bartley, Abel A. *Keeping the Faith: Race, Politics, and Social Development in Jacksonville, Florida, 1940–1970.* Westport, Conn.: Greenwood Press, 2000.

Bay, Mia. *To Tell the Truth Freely: The Life of Ida B. Wells.* New York: Hill and Wang, 2009.

Beatty, Bess. "John Willis Menard: A Progressive Black in Post-Civil War Florida," *Florida Historical Quarterly* 59 (October 1980): 123–43.

Bentley, George R. *A History of the Freedmen's Bureau.* Philadelphia: University of Pennsylvania, 1955.

Blight, David W. *Race and Reunion.* Cambridge, MA: Harvard University Press, 2001.

Brown, Canter, Jr. *Florida's Black Public Officials, 1867–1924.* Tuscaloosa: University of Alabama Press, 1998.

Brown, Canter, Jr. *Ossian Bingley Hart, Florida's Loyalist Reconstruction Governor.* Baton Rouge: Louisiana State University Press, 1997.

Brown, Canter, Jr. "'Where are now the hopes I cherished?' The Life and Times of Robert Meacham." *Florida Historical Quarterly* 69 (July 1990): 1–36.

Brown, Canter, Jr., and Larry E. Rivers. *For a Great and Grand Purpose: The Beginnings of the AMEZ Church in Florida, 1864–1905.* Gainesville: University Press of Florida, 2004.

Brown, Lois. *Encyclopedia of the Harlem Literary Renaissance.* New York: Facts on File, Inc., 2006.

Burnett, Gene M. *Florida's Past: People and Events that Shaped the State, Volume 1.* Sarasota, FL: Pineapple Press, 1986.

Carle, Susan, "The Lawyer's Role in a Contemporary Democracy, Promoting Social Change and Political Values, Debunking the Myth of Civil Rights Liberalism: Visions of Racial Justice in the Thought of T. Thomas Fortune, 1880–1890." *Fordham Law Review,* vol. 77, issue 4 (2009): 1479–1533.

Catalogue of the Officers and Students of Howard University from June 1874 to February 1876. Washington, D. C.: O. H. Reed, 1876.

Catalogue of the Officers and Students of Howard University from March 1876 to March 1878. Washington, D. C.: W. M. Stuart, 1878.

Cimbala, Paul A. *The Freedmen's Bureau: Reconstructing the American South after the Civil War.* Malabar, FL: Krieger Publishing Company, 2005.

Clark, James C. "John Wallace and the Writing of Reconstruction History." *Florida Historical Quarterly* 67 (April 1989): 409–27.

Clinton, Catherine. *The Plantation Mistress.* New York: Pantheon Books, 1982.

Cochran, Thomas Everette. *History of Public-School Education in Florida,* Lancaster, PA: Press of the New Era Printing Company, 1921.

Cox, Dale A. *The Battle of Marianna, Florida.* Fort Smith: Dale Cox, Publisher, 2007.

Davis, Thomas Frederick, *History of Jacksonville, Florida and Vicinity: 1513 to 1924.* St. Augustine, FL: Florida Historical Society, 1925; reprint ed., Gainesville: University of Florida Press, 1964.

Davis, William Watson. *The Civil War and Reconstruction in Florida.* New York: Columbia University Press, 1913; reprint ed., Gainesville: University of Florida Press, 1964.

Derby, George, and James T. White. *The National Cyclopaedia of American Biography, Volume XIV.* New York, James T. White Co., 1910.

Detweiler, Frederick G. *The Negro Press in the United States.* Chicago: University of Chicago Press, 1922.

Dickens, Rita. *Marse Ned: The Story of an Old Southern Family.* New York: Exposition Press, 1958.

Dodd, Dorothy. "'Bishop' Pearce and the Reconstruction of Leon County." *Apalachee* 2 (1946): 5–12.

DuBois, W. E. B. *Black Reconstruction in America, 1860–1880.* New York, Atheneum, 1935.

DuBois, W. E. B. "The Freedmen's Bureau." *Atlantic Monthly* 87 (March 1901), 354–65.

Dunster, Alfreda M. *Crusade for Justice: The Autobiography of Ida B. Wells,* Chicago: University of Chicago Press, 1970.

Farmer-Kaiser, Mary. *Freedwomen and the Freedmen's Bureau: Race, Gender, and*

Public Policy in the Age of Emancipation. New York: Fordham University Press, 2010.

Fortune, Timothy Thomas. *Black and White: Land, Labor, and Politics in the South*. New York: Fords, Howard, & Hubert, 1884.

Fortune, Timothy Thomas. *Dreams of Life: Miscellaneous Poems*. New York: published by the author, 1905.

Fortune, Timothy Thomas. *The Negro in Politics: Some Pertinent Reflections on the Past and Present Political Status of the Afro-American, Together with a Cursory Investigation into the Motives Which Actuate Partisan Organizations*. New York: Ogilvie and Rowntree, 1886.

Franklin, John Hope, and August Meier, eds. *Black Leaders of the Twentieth Century*. Urbana: University of Illinois Press, 1982.

Gibbs, Mifflin Wistar. *Shadow and Light: An Autobiography with Reminiscences of the Last and Present Century*. Washington, DC, 1902.

Giddings, Joshua R. *The Exiles of Florida*. Columbus, Ohio: Follett, Foster and Company, 1858.

Goodell, William. *Slavery and Anti-Slavery; A History of the Great Struggle in Both Hemispheres; with a View of the Slavery Question in the United States*. New York: William Goodell, 1853.

Hancock, Harold B. "The Status of the Negro in Delaware after the Civil War, 1865–1875," *Delaware History*, vol. XIII, No. 1 (April 1968), 56–66.

Harlan, Louis R. *Booker T. Washington: The Wizard of Tuskegee, 1901–1915*. New York: Oxford University Press, 1983.

Harlan, Louis R. and Raymond W. Smock, eds. *The Booker T. Washington Papers, V*. Urbana: University of Illinois Press, 1976.

Harris, Joel Chandler. *The Chronicles of Aunt Minervy Ann*. New York: Charles Scribner's Sons, 1899.

Hentz, Charles A. *The Autobiography of Dr. C. A. Hentz, Florida and North Carolina, 1827–1894*, Vol. II, Originals on file in the Southern Historical Collection, University of North Carolina Library, Chapel Hill.

Hiller, Amy M. "The Disenfranchisement of Delaware Negroes in the Late Nineteenth Century." *Delaware History*, vol. XIII, No. 2 (October 1968), 124–53.

Johnson, James Weldon. *Along This Way: The Autobiography of James Weldon Johnson*. New York: Viking Penguin, 1933; reprint ed., New York: Penguin Group, 1990.

Jones, Maxine D. and Kevin M. McCarthy. *African Americans in Florida*. Sarasota, Fla.: Pineapple Press, 1993.

Kenney, Patricia L. "LaVilla, Florida, 1866–1887: Reconstruction Dreams and the Formation of a Black Community" in *The African American Heritage of Florida*. ed. by David L. Colburn and Jane L. Landers. Gainesville: University Press of Florida, 1995.

Klingman, Peter D. *Josiah Walls: Florida's Black Congressman of Reconstruction*. Gainesville: University of Florida Press, 1976.

Logan, Rayford W. *Howard University, The First Hundred Years 1967–1967.* New York: NYU Press, 1969.

Lovett, Bobby L. *The African American History of Nashville, Tennessee, 1790–1930: Elites and Dilemmas*. Fayetteville: University of Arkansas Press, 1999.

McFeely, William S. *Grant: A Biography*. New York: W. W. Norton & Co., 1981.

Menard, Edith. "John Willis Menard, First Negro Elected to the U.S. Congress, First Negro to Speak in the U.S. Congress." *Negro History Bulletin* 28. December 1964, 53–54.

Murray, Vince. "Captain J. J. Dickison: Marion County's Civil War Hero." Ocala *Star-Banner*. April 25, 2008. Available online at http://www.ocala.com/article/20080425/OCALACOMHISTORY/101010039

Neyland, Ledell W. and John W. Riley. *The History of Florida Agricultural and Mechanical University*. Gainesville: University of Florida Press, 1963.

Patterson, Tiffany Ruby. *Zora Neale Hurston and a History of Southern Life*. Philadelphia: Temple University Press, 2005.

Penn, Garland I. *The Afro-American Press, and Its Editors*. Springfield, MA: Willey & Co., 1891.

Porter, Kenneth W. "The Episode of Osceola's Wife." *Florida Historical Quarterly* 26 (July 1947): 92–98.

Purdee, Armstrong. "Eye-Witness Tells of Burning of Church," *Kalendar*. Men's Club, St. Luke's Episcopal Church, Marianna, Florida. June 1, 1931. Available online at http://www.rootsweb.ancestry.com/~flgatsaa/kalendar.html, accessed on Dec. 31, 2013.

Richardson, Joe M. "Christian Abolitionism: The American Missionary Association and the Florida Negro." *The Journal of Negro Education* 40 (Winter 1971): 35–44.

Richardson, Joe M. "The Freedmen's Bureau and Negro Education in Florida." *Journal of Negro Education* 31 (Autumn 1962), 460–67.

Richardson, Joe. M. *The Negro in the Reconstruction of Florida, 1876–1877.* Tallahassee: Florida State University Press, 1965; reprint ed., Tampa: Trend House, 1973.

Rivers, Larry E. "'He Treats His Fellow Man Properly': Building Community in Multi-Cultural Florida," in *Amid Political, Cultural, and Civic Diversity: Building a Sense of Statewide Community in Florida*. ed. by Lance deHaven-Smith and David Colburn. Dubuque, Iowa: Kendall/Hunt, 1998.

Rivers, Larry E. *Rebels and Runaways: Slave Resistance in Florida*. Urbana: University of Illinois Press, 2012.

Rivers, Larry E. *Slavery in Florida: Territorial Days to Emancipation*. Gainesville: University Press of Florida, 2000.

Rivers, Larry E., and Canter Brown Jr. "'The Art of Gathering a Crowd': Florida's Pat Chappelle and the Origins of Black-Owned Vaudeville." *Journal of African American History* 92 (Spring 2007), 169–90.

Rivers, Larry E., and Canter Brown Jr. "John Willis Menard and *Lays in Summer Lands*" in John Willis Menard, *Lays in Summer Land*, ed. by Larry E. Rivers, Richard Mathews, and Canter Brown Jr. Tampa: University of Tampa Press, 2002.

Rivers, Larry E., and Canter Brown Jr. *Laborers in the Vineyard of the Lord: The Beginnings of the AME Church in Florida, 1865–1895*. Gainesville: University Press of Florida, 2001.

Rivers, Larry E., and Canter Brown Jr. "A Monument to the Progress of the Race; The Intellectual and Political Origins of the Florida Agricultural and Mechanical University, 1865–1887." *Florida Historical Quarterly* 85 (Summer 2006): 1–41.

Royster, Jacqueline Jones, ed. *Southern Horrors and Other Writings: The Anti-Lynching Campaign of Ida B. Wells, 1892–1900*. Boston: Bedford/St. Martin's Press, 1997.

Seraile, William. "Theophilus G. Steward, Intellectual Chaplain, 25th US Colored Infantry." *Nebraska History* 66 (1985), 272–93.

Shofner, Jerrell H. *Jackson County, Florida—A History*. Marianna: Jackson County Heritage Association, 1985.

Shofner, Jerrell H. *Nor Is It over Yet: Florida in the Era of Reconstruction 1863–1877.* Gainesville: University of Florida Press, 1974.

Shuften, John T. *A Colored Man's Exposition of the Acts and Doings of the Radical Party of the South, From 1865 to 1876, And Its Probable Overthrow By President Hayes' Southern Policy*. Jacksonville, Fla.: Gibson & Dennis, 1877.

Simmons, William J. *Men of Mark: Eminent, Progressive and Rising*. Cleveland: Geo. M. Rewell & Co., 1887.

Simon, John Y., ed. *The Papers of Ulysses S. Grant, Volume 26: 1875*. Carbondale, IL: Southern Illinois University Press, 2003.

Sitiki. *The Odyssey of an African Slave*. ed. Patricia C. Griffin. Gainesville: University Press of Florida, 2009.

Smith, Jessie Carney, ed. *Notable Black Women, Book II*. Detroit: Gale Research Inc., 1996.

Smith, Julia Floyd. *Slavery and Plantation Growth in Antebellum Florida, 1821–1860*. Gainesville: University of Florida Press, 1973.

Stanley, J. Randall. *History of Jackson County Florida*. Marianna, FL: Jackson County Historical Society, 1950.

Suggs, Henry Lewis, ed. *The Black Press in the South, 1865–1979*. Westport, Conn.: Greenwood Press, 1983.

Taylor, Susie King. *Reminiscences of My Life: A Black Woman's Civil War Memoirs*, ed. by Patricia W. Romero and Willie Lee Rose. New York: Markus Wiener Publishing, 1988.

Taylor, Susie King. *Reminiscences of My Life in Camp: An African American Woman's Civil War Memoirs*. Athens: University of Georgia Press, 2006.

Tobier, Nina, ed. *Voices of Sag Harbor: A Village Remembered*. New York: Friends of the John Jermain Memorial Library, 2007.

Thornbrough, Emma Lou. *T. Thomas Fortune: Militant Journalist*. Chicago: University of Chicago Press, 1972.

Turner, Gregg M. *A Journey into Florida Railroad History*. Gainvesville: University of Florida Press, 2008.

Wallace, John. *Carpetbag Rule in Florida: The Inside Workings of the Reconstruction of Civil Government in Florida After the Close of the Civil War*. Jacksonville: Da Costa Printing and Publishing House, 1888, Reprint. Kennesaw, Ga.: Continental Book Co., 1959.

Washington, Booker T. *The Negro in Business*. Boston: Hertel, Jenkins & Co., 1907.

Weinfeld, Daniel R. *The Jackson County War: Reconstruction and Resistance in Post-Civil War Florida*. Tuscaloosa: University of Alabama Press, 2012.

Weinfeld, Daniel R. "'More Courage than Discretion': Charles M. Hamilton in Reconstruction-Era Florida." *Florida Historical Quarterly* 84 (Spring 2006): 479–516.

Weinfeld, Daniel R. "Samuel Fleishman: Tragedy in Reconstruction-Era Florida." *Southern Jewish History* 8 (2005): 31–75.

Whyte, James H. *The Uncivil War: Washington During the Reconstruction, 1865–1878*. Washington, DC: Twayne Publishers, 1958.

Wickman, Patricia R. *Osceola's Legacy*. Tuscaloosa: University of Alabama Press, 2006.

Williamson, Edward C. *Florida Politics during the Gilded Age, 1877–1893*. Gainesville: University of Presses of Florida, 1976.

Woolsey, Nathan. "Butler Was First Republican Sheriff." *Santa Rosa Press Gazette*. 6 Nov. 1992.

Works Progress Administration (WPA). *Slave Narratives Project*, Vol. 3, Florida. Washington, DC: Government Printing Office, 1941.

Young, Darius J. "Henry S. Harmon: Pioneer African American Attorney in Reconstruction-era Florida." *Florida Historical Quarterly* 85 (Fall 2006): 177–96.

Unpublished

Coles, David J. "Far from the Fields of Glory: Military Operations in Florida during the Civil War." PhD Dissertation, Florida State University, 1996.

Goodwin, Gary B. "Joseph E. Lee of Jacksonville, 1880–1920." Master's thesis. Florida State University, 1996.

John Q. Dickinson Collection, Bailey/Howe Library, University of Vermont.

Mounter, Michael R. "Richard Theodore Greener: The Idealist, Statesman, Scholar, and South Carolinian." PhD Dissertation, University of South Carolina, 2002.

Richardson, Barbara Ann. "A History of Blacks in Jacksonville, Florida, 1860–1895; A Socio-Economic Study." PhD Dissertation. Carnegie-Mellon University, 1975.

Rivers, Larry Eugene and Canter Brown Jr., "Attorney John Wallace: Pioneering the Profession of Law within Florida's African American Community" (under consideration for publication, *Journal of the Georgia Association of Historians*).

Williams, Learotha. "'A Wider Field of Usefulness': The Life and Times of Jonathan Clarkson Gibbs, c. 1828–1874." PhD Dissertation. Florida State University, 2003.

Government Publications

Journal of the Proceedings of the Assembly of the State of Florida, 1868–1873.

Journal of Proceedings of the House of Representatives of the General Assembly of the State of Florida at its Thirteenth Session, 1864.

Journal of the Proceedings of the Senate of the State of Florida, 1869–1873.

Records of the Assistant Commissioner and Subordinate field offices for the State of Florida, Bureau of Refugees, Freedmen, and Abandoned Lands 1865–1872 (microform), Department of Special Collections, Smathers Library, University of Florida, Gainesville.

United States Census, 1830, 1860, 1870, 1880.

United States Congress Serial Set. Washington, DC. "Testimony Taken by the Joint Select Committee to Inquire Into the Condition of Affairs in the Late Insurrectionary States." House Report No. 22, pt. 13, 42d Congress, 2d sess., 1872.

United States House of Representatives, 42nd Cong., 2d Sess., Misc. Doc. 34, pp. 65–67.

Newspapers and Periodicals

American Anti-Slavery Almanac (1839)

Cleveland Gazette, 1897.

Dallas Morning News, 1894.

Fernandina Florida Mirror, 1881.

New York Age, 1889–1891, 1913.

New York Freeman, 1885, 1886.

New York Sun, 1880, 1897.

New York Times, 1900.

Norfolk Journal and Guide, 1927, 1928.

Philadelphia North American and United States Gazette, 1872.

Philadelphia Tribune, 1927.

The Quarterly Anti-Slavery Magazine, vol. II, (July 1837).
Rutland (VT) *Daily Herald*, 1869.
Santa Rosa Press Gazette, 1992.
Tallahassee Weekly Floridian, 1869, 1871.
Topeka (KS) *Plaindealer*, 1928.
Washington Post, 1909.
Washington (DC) *National Republican*, 1876.

Websites

www.familysearch.org
www.findagrave.com
National Park Service, Civil War Soldiers and Sailors System. http://www.itd.nps.gov/cwss
United States Coast Guard. http://www.uscg.mil/History/faqs/BIO_Sumner_Kimball.html.
United States Department of Commerce, National Oceanic and Atmospheric Administration, Atlantic Oceanographic and Meteorological Library. http://www.aoml.noaa.gov/hrd/hurdat/figs_tables.htm

Manuscripts

Dickinson, John Q. Letter to Isaac Dickinson. April 11, 1869. Special Collections. Bailey/Howe Library, University of Vermont.
Dickinson, John Q. "Memoranda of Occurrences relating to the assassinations in Jackson County September 28th 1869 & following." Deanne and Arnold Kaplan Collection of Early American Judaica.
Philips, Ethelred. Letters to James J. Philips. August 2, 1865 & Dec. 19, 1866. James J. Philips Papers. Southern Historical Collection, University of North Carolina, Chapel Hill, North Carolina.

Index